Poulenc's Songs: An Analysis of Style

Poulenc's Songs:
An Analysis of Style

VIVIAN LEE POATES WOOD

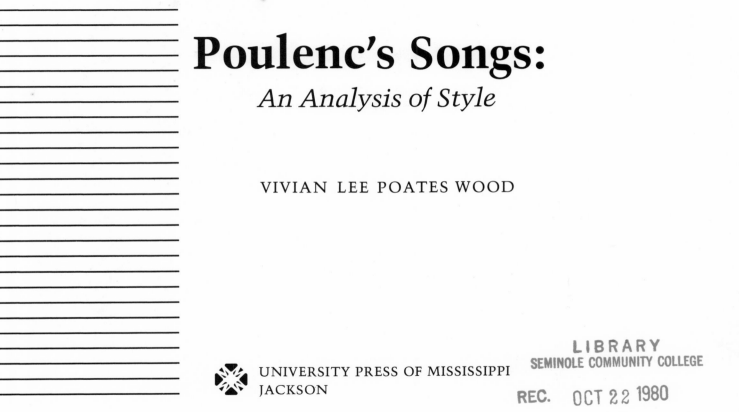

UNIVERSITY PRESS OF MISSISSIPPI
JACKSON

Copyright © 1979 by the University Press of Mississippi
Manufactured in the United States of America
All Rights Reserved
Designed by James J. Johnson

*This volume is sponsored by the
University of Southern Mississippi*

Library of Congress Cataloging in Publication Data
Wood, Vivian Lee Poates.

  Poulenc's songs: an analysis of style

  Bibliography: p.
  Includes indexes.
    1. Poulenc, Francis, 1899–1963. Songs.   I. Title.
MT115.P68W6   784'.3'00924   78–14532
ISBN 0–87805–086–8

Dedicated to the Memory of My Grandparents
Rosa Lee Poates & Edward Francis Wood

Table of Contents

Foreword

Vivian Wood's study on Francis Poulenc's songs is not the first publication about this composer. Several books have been written about Poulenc's life and his music; one even deals with the interpretation of his songs for the performer. However, the technical aspects of the songs such as melodic and harmonic structure and form have not yet been examined in detail. The present volume, though scholarly, is not a dry analytical essay. The author's love for the music permeates the discussions and her empathy with the literary and sociological background of the texts is apparent.

Esthetic value judgments are kept at a minimum. Still, objectivity does not prevent genuine appreciation of the melodic gift of the composer on wide varying emotional levels.

The reader will achieve fuller understanding of Poulenc's lovely lyrical output.

Paul A. Pisk
Hollywood, California, 1978

Preface

The songs of Francis Poulenc have held for me, a singer, both fascination and challenge. In them is an unending variety of musical style, humor and drama, lyric inventiveness, harmonic color, and a superb understanding of poetic intent. The composer does not evoke positive opinions from all sides. Much criticism has been heaped upon Poulenc by reviewers who see him as often superficial and a captive of the café and dance halls, a man with scant regard for the formalities of structure and development: "Poulenc has proved himself the essence of elegance and polish in a number of works which are rather higher than salon music, but approach it very nearly . . . and in this regard they have their value . . . and he may be said to illustrate one aspect of the French goût in its purest form."[1]

A closer study of the songs of Poulenc, however, reveals that he thoroughly understood his craft. Structure there is, though not in the style or spirit of the famous German Lieder composers such as Schubert, Schumann, Brahms, and Hugo Wolf.

Despite the accepted fact that Poulenc was a superb song composer, that his style

---

1. Norman Demuth, *Musical Trends in the 20th Century* (London: Rockliff, 1952), 72.

was totally individualistic, that he had a unique understanding of the poetry he set to music, and although many of his songs appear internationally on concert programs and have achieved performances by most of the great contemporary recitalists, there has been, so far, no detailed study of his vocal solos.

In universities and conservatories, German Lieder and the songs of such French composers as Debussy, Fauré, and Ravel are taught as standard repertory material. *Le Bestiaire, Banalités*, and the cycle *Tel Jour Telle Nuit* of Poulenc have moved into recital programs, but the bulk of Poulenc's songs are not sung in this country. This fact determined the purpose of this study: not only to analyze the songs, probe their harmonies and melodic structure, their form and their poetry, but to offer it to singers, especially Americans, in the hope that they will appreciate this twentieth-century master. If they do, they will find a kindred spirit, a man of immense sensitivity who lived intensely but with humor, and who shared his passions and visions through that individuality which made his music, especially his songs, a personal and universal statement.

One cannot approach a study of Francis Poulenc without acknowledgment of the work of his biographer, Henri Hell, whose book *Francis Poulenc* was translated into English by Edward Lockspeiser. Interviews by journalists, sections of other books, and critical music reviews reveal added data, but the Hell book must stand as the most comprehensive source of information on the composer. Because of its scope, it is necessarily limited in detailed compositional analysis, except for specific examples, but it is used here as a main source of biographical reference.

Poulenc's admonition to seek first to understand the poetry is essential. Therefore, a companion book is planned to discuss the poetry stylistically. Coauthor is Denise Restout, author of "Landowska On Music" (New York: Stein and Day, 1964), who is also the director of the Wanda Landowska Center and an internationally recognized harpsichordist and teacher. It was Denise Restout who originally inspired this book when she shared her personal experiences and remembrances of Francis Poulenc and made available notebooks and letters from Poulenc to Wanda Landowska.

Gratitude is also extended to Dr. Paul A. Pisk, eminent composer, pianist, teacher, and musicologist, without whom this undertaking would not have been started or completed. His generosity in writing the Foreword has enriched this book.

Also, Ada L. Stillman, who gave lavishly of her time and vast knowledge of the French language and the French art song, must be recognized on behalf of the many professional singers and students in New York who received her help and inspiration.

Vivian Wood
Munich, Germany, 1979

Poulenc's Songs: An Analysis of Style

I Background & Biography

Secular song has deep roots in French soil. "Hora vos dic ver raizun,"[1] from the eleventh century, is the earliest extant example of the Provençal song preceding the great flowering of the troubadours and trouvères during the twelfth and thirteenth centuries. A vocal line, accompanied by instruments, was characteristic of the fourteenth-century secular song literature. The names of Machaut, Dufay, Binchois, and others are affixed to some of the great songs in rondeau and virelai forms. The last half of the fifteenth century witnessed the development of the French polyphonic chanson. Josquin, Compère, and La Rue achieved fame for works that evolved into characteristically witty and elegant songs. With the rise of monody, the polyphonic chanson disappeared from the literature. The baroque air de cour, pastourelle, bergerette, brunette, and romance appeared in the seventeenth and eighteenth centuries. In the nineteenth century the secular type with which we are concerned emerged.

The "romance" portended the rebirth of French song writing. It greatly influenced Hector Berlioz and Charles Gounod. Berlioz is credited with christening the French art song "mélodie,"[2] and he and Gounod are responsible for the reawakening of song literature in nineteenth-century France.

The French, explicit in language, have two words—"mélodie" and "chanson"—to designate clearly the differences in compositions for voice and piano set to French texts. "Mélodie" is used for the serious song referred to as the "Lied" in German. "Chanson" also is applied to recital songs, but when the composer calls a composition "chanson" he is indicating an implied popular style such as café music or music with a folk song flavor. Sometimes, "chanson" appears as part of a poet's title and the musical style is that of the "mélodie." Then, to the French, it is a "mélodie."

Franck, Chabrier, Chausson, Duparc, Fauré, Debussy, and Ravel brought the French art song to greatness. Francis Poulenc is heir to this tradition. His compositional techniques are designed to follow the French poem in nuance, construction, and spirit, and poets do not adhere to consistent principles of conventional musical form. This fact alone was enough to intrigue and incite a curiosity about how Poulenc could achieve in his songs what Henri Hell has called "the most significant department of his work."[3]

In 1935, the great singer Pierre Bernac began a long association with Poulenc, who chose him as a partner in hundreds of performances of his songs. Bernac has written:

> Beyond all doubt, most of Francis Poulenc's finest work was in the field of vocal composition—choral works, lyrical works, and melodies. His inspiration never flowed more spontaneously than when stimulated by a literary text. He had an exceptional feeling for French declamatory style, and his melodic gift, which was the very essence of his music,

inspired him to find the appropriate musical line to heighten the expression of the literary phrase. To quote his own words: "The musical setting of a poem should be an act of love, never a marriage of convenience." And again: "I have never claimed to achieve the musical resolution of poetic problems by means of intelligence; the voices of the heart and of instinct are far more reliable."[4]

Martin Cooper links Poulenc's style to the strength of his individuality:

Francis Poulenc's musical personality has no precedent in musical history; and that his personality predominated in the music usually attributed to Les Six generally is shown by the fact that he alone has continued to write in a style that has no doubt developed greater solidity, but is still recognizably the same as that which shocked or amused Paris—and very soon all Europe and America—in the years following the first war.[5]

Warren Kent Warner, in his excellent harmonic Poulenc study, describes Poulenc's style as "eclectic, in the best sense of that much-used word."

Impressionism, neo-classicism, and neo-romanticism are present in recognizable amounts, all making substantial contributions to the harmonic, melodic and rhythmic texture of his music. Yet, in spite of these obvious derivations, few twentieth-century composers present a style as unmistakably identifiable, as uniquely personal as Poulenc's. His music, happily, absorbs the many contributing flavors, without losing its own identity.[6]

5 **Background & Biography**

Perhaps those who have found such beauty in these songs share Pierre Bernac's admonishment in the introduction to his *The Interpretation of French Song*: "This book is not written by a musicologist, and indeed it is not from the angle of musicology or musical analysis that the study of the interpretation of the French mélodie is here approached, or should be approached! It is written by an interpreter, whose only wish is to offer the benefit of his experience to those singers who wish to explore an enchanting realm of song."[7] In the face of this statement from so eminent an authority, this writer has undertaken exactly what Bernac has counseled against. Perhaps it is because, as an American and as a teacher of young American singers, I find that such a study is necessary. To the French, Francis Poulenc does not need to be explained. To Americans, however, he is formidable because of the poetry of his songs, his style of composition, and his entirely "French" individuality.

In 1920, French critic Henri Collet gave the name "Groupe des Six" to a band of revolutionary composers—Darius Milhaud, Arthur Honegger, Louis Durey, Germaine Tailleferre, Georges Auric, and Poulenc. There are conflicting accounts concerning the exact place where the concerts that prompted this christening were heard, but there is no question as to who the composers were or their artistic intent. Hell describes the beginnings of the "Groupe des Six":

> A cellist, Felix Delgrange, took the new composers of the day under his wing and organised concerts of their works in a humble studio in . . . Montparnasse. . . .
> The famous *Groupe des Six* came into being from these Delgrange concerts. After

one of the concerts the critic Henri Collet wrote two articles in *Comoedia*, the first entitled "The Five Russians, the Six Frenchmen and Satie" and the second "The Six Frenchmen."[8]

Norman Demuth notes that the formation of the group was accidental, arising through a casual meeting in 1916 between Darius Milhaud and Arthur Honegger at the studio of the poet Blaise Cendrars. Also present were Erik Satie, Germaine Tailleferre, and Louis Durey. "It was suggested by Cendrars that a number of concerts devoted to the works of young composers would be a good thing, and Erik Satie remarked that instead of following the example of other societies and playing other people's works, they would concentrate on their own." Demuth adds, "This proved a popular suggestion in every way and as time went on the party was joined by Jean Cocteau . . . the poet and dramatist and another composer, Francis Poulenc . . . . The composite group took on the name of the 'Nouveaux Jeunes.'"[9]

Darius Milhaud offers this account of "Les Six":

Delgrange abandoned the cello to devote himself wholly to the cause of the new art; he organized concerts in a little hall in Montparnasse, the Salle Huyghens; the backless benches were uncomfortable and the atmosphere was unbreathable because of the fumes of the stove, but all that was elegant in Parisian society, as well as the artists and devotees of the new music, rubbed shoulders there. Jane (née Jeanne) Bathori and Ricardo Viñes, the faithful pioneers, the (Female) Capelle Quartet, the pianists Juliette Meerovitch and Marcelle Meyer, and the actor Pierre Bertin who also sang, lent us their devoted help and disinterested services. There was also a very important center of intellectual activity, placed under the aegis of Shakespeare and of contemporary literature, in the two neighboring bookshops of Adrienne Monnier and Sylvia Beach in the rue de l'Odéon. . . .

After a concert at the Salle Huyghens, at which Bertin sang Louis Durey's "Images à Crusoe" on words by Saint-Léger Léger, and the Capelle Quartet played my Fourth Quartet, the Critic Henri Collet published in *Comoedia* a chronicle entitled "Five Russians and Six Frenchmen." Quite arbitrarily he had chosen six names: Auric, Durey, Honegger, Poulenc, Tailleferre, and my own, merely because we knew one another, were good friends and had figured on the same programs; quite irrespective of our different temperaments and wholly dissimilar characters.[10]

Two years before, Jean Cocteau had shocked Paris with a scathing attack against Wagner, Debussy, Rimsky-Korsakov, and Mussorgsky, in his article "Le Coq et l'Arlequin," written in defense of Erik Satie and Pablo Picasso, with whom he had collaborated to produce *Parade*, the ballet mounted by Serge de Diaghilev and the Russian Ballet in Paris in May, 1917, at the Théâtre du Châtebet. New forces were challenging the traditional, capturing the public's ear and eye. Before personal and artistic differences parted them, "Les Six" had "provided a much needed breath of fresh air in the stuffy, over-heated atmosphere of French music of the time. Contemporary music was brought more nearly into accord with the times. . . . French music was out of the harmonic jungle of the past quarter-century."[11]

How, specifically, did Francis Poulenc reach the stage of development which could propel him at the age of eighteen into the limelight as the youngest member of this "Groupe des Six"? How did he find himself in the company of these artistic rebels who were challenging the traditionalists in open warfare against Wagnerian and Debussian influences?

At 2 Place des Saussaies in Paris, January 7, 1899, Francis Poulenc was born to Emile and Jenny (Royer) Poulenc. Emile Poulenc was a wealthy industrialist who was to provide his son with the security of financial independence and a devout Roman Catholic lineage. Jenny Poulenc's pious roots did not run so deep, though she was also of Catholic heritage. Her family, for generations, had been cabinet-makers, bronze-founders, and tapestry-weavers in the finest sense of those crafts. She was a talented pianist and interested in the theatrical and musical trends of contemporary Paris. Through her brother, who was devoted to the theater, Jenny Poulenc was kept aware of the events of this art and, as a young boy, Francis was influenced by this interest of his mother's. In Poulenc's music, the sharp division between his secular and sacred works, which almost sets up an alternating pattern, has been recognized. Asked about this contrast between the deeply serious and devout religious music as opposed to the often erotic, sensuous, and music hall character of some of his secular music, Poulenc said:

> It has all to do with an artist's view of life and also to a great extent, with his upbringing. You see, my father was a devout Catholic and it was from him that I inherited my religious inspiration. In fact, I had a great-uncle, the Abbé Joseph Poulenc who was the curé of

Background & Biography

Ivry-sur-Seine, so that a strong religious tradition is firmly tied to my work. It was from my mother, on the other hand, that I inherited my great love for music; she was a delightful pianist with excellent musical taste. I recall being completely enthralled when she played Schubert, Mozart, Chopin and Schumann. I was also inspired by some of the lesser composers in my mother's repertoire, such as Massenet, Grieg and Anton Rubinstein.

I am certain that it was my mother who inspired me to write my "mauvaise musique." It was also my mother's part of the family that kept abreast of the entire artistic world; my uncle Papoum introduced me to my love for the theatre, and it was from him I learned about Réjane, Sarah Bernhardt and the like. So it is really not surprising that there is a duality in myself as well as in my music.[12]

Poulenc's formal musical training consisted mainly of study of the piano. His mother saw that his lessons started in his fifth year, and by the time he was eight years old he studied with Boutet de Monvel. He was prodigious and in 1915 began work with Ricardo Viñes who significantly influenced his career. This Spanish pianist was forty years old when the young Poulenc began his studies. Through him, Poulenc met Eric Satie, Georges Auric, and the singer Jeanne Bathori. Viñes was a passionate interpreter of new French and Spanish contemporary music, and a member of the inner circle of Parisian performers. Poulenc had met Viñes through a family friend, Geneviève Sienkiewicz, and for his audition he played Schumann's *Faschingsschwank* and Préludes of Debussy, including *Minstrels*.

Poulenc recalls that Viñes "would kick me in the shins whenever I was clumsy at the pedals. . . . No one could teach the art of using the pedals . . . an essential feature of modern piano music . . . better than Viñes. He somehow managed to extract clarity precisely from the ambiguities of the pedals." How well the lesson of the pedals stayed with Poulenc may be judged by his following remarks made during an interview in New York in 1960: "If one does not use a great deal of pedal . . . again, all is lost. I insist: If one avoids using the pedal, there is no use . . . it will be another composer he is playing. I count on the pedal as a cook counts on cream to bind his sauce."[13]

Viñes was a master of the interpretation of Fauré, Debussy, and Ravel, and contributed heavily to the formation of Poulenc's taste as well as his piano technique. Poulenc has said, "I owe him everything."[14]

It should be mentioned, too, that Jeanne Bathori and Raymonde Linassier were important influences during this time. Bathori was a fine singer who had introduced many songs of Fauré, Debussy, Ravel, and Satie to Paris. It was through her friendship with Viñes that the young Poulenc met Arthur Honegger, and his ever-widening musical acquaintances soon included Germaine Tailleferre and Louis Durey.

Raymonde Linassier and Poulenc had been children together. She opened the doors to the world of writers and poets, introducing Poulenc to the works of Claudel and Gide, Proust and Joyce, Verlaine, Mallarmé, and Baudelaire. She was to become a barrister at the Paris Court of Appeal and was also an archaeologist at the Musée Guimet. Her deep literary interest and her love of poetry were shared with Poulenc during his years of adolescence and early manhood. The two were constant companions in Paris, often seen in Left Bank bookstores. It was Raymonde Linassier who took Poulenc to the "Aux Amis des Livres," a shop owned by Adrienne Monnier, which was the meeting place for Valéry, Gide, Claudel, Joyce, Larbaud, Apollinaire, and Fargue. Here, Poulenc made fast friends with André Breton, Louis Aragon, and Paul Eluard, whose poems he would later set to music. Poulenc and Linassier enjoyed an intimate friendship until her death in 1932. His ballet *Les Animaux modèles* was dedicated to her memory.

Influences of his boyhood and adolescence can be traced through the music to which he devoted himself as a young pianist. Debussy had been an early hero, and when Poulenc was only eight years old the *Danse sacrée et danse profane*, for harp and string orchestra, had overwhelmed him. As Hell says, "his one desire was to be able to find for himself the intriguing chords of the ninth in this work at the piano. . . . This passion for Debussy was steadily to develop, though he was hardly able to play any of the piano works before the age of fourteen."[15]

A similar emotional response was accorded Poulenc's discovery of Schubert's *Winterreise* in a music store in Fontainebleau when he was eleven years old. He is said to have played the songs of this cycle over and over that day, finding "Die Krähe," "Der Lindenbaum," "Der Leiermann," and "Die Nebensonnen" especially moving.

Stravinsky's *Firebird*, *Petruchka*, and *Le Sacre du Printemps*, all of which he had heard before he was fifteen years old, excited the young Poulenc and even set him at odds with his father who did not appreciate his taste. Not listed in any catalogue of works are Poulenc's boyhood compositions, which were generally stylistic copies of Debussy and Stravinsky. He was proud of his piano piece *Processional for the Cremation of a Mandarin*, modeled on the Chinese March from Stravinsky's *Nightingale*, a portent of his later exoticism.

The first entry in a catalogue of Poulenc's compositions is a work for voice. It was an instant success. Poulenc discovered a volume called "Les Poésies de Makoko Kangourou," which was attributed to a Negro poet. In France in 1917, French musicians and writers were trying to assimilate Negro art and music. As it turned out, the poem was a hoax. Poulenc, nevertheless, titled this setting for baritone, piano, and string quartet *Rhapsodie Nègre*. It was first performed on December 11, 1917, as a part of a series of concerts of contemporary music sponsored by Poulenc's friend Jeanne Bathori at the Théâtre du Vieux-Colombier.

Even though, at the last minute, Poulenc had to sing the songs himself, because the baritone found them too difficult, the performance was a tremendous success, and the eighteen-year-old was known to Parisians overnight as an exciting new talent. The impact of this recognition was reflected in the response of Diaghilev, who was so impressed that he talked of commissioning Poulenc to write a ballet. Stravinsky immediately introduced him to his London publisher; Ravel also encouraged Poulenc, but urged him to further his technical training. The public appreciation was so great that *Rhapsodie Nègre* was performed soon again during the series.

A month later, however, Poulenc was called to the army and served in an antiaircraft unit in the Vosges on the Western Front. He remained a soldier after the armistice, serving out his military commitment until October, 1921, though he managed to make many trips to Paris.

During his service Poulenc wrote *Sonata for piano duet* and *Mouvements perpétuels*; Ricardo Viñes played this in Paris in 1919 and it was well received. These works were, compared with Satie and the eighteenth-century harpsichordists, "spiced with twentieth-century notions of dissonance."[16]

In 1960, Poulenc evaluated these pieces in retrospect and made a pertinent comparison with the piano writing in his songs:

> My compositions for piano solo are, alas, my weakest! To make matters worse, there are quite a lot of them . . . my "Mouvements perpetuels, Impromptus, Novelettes, Improvisations," etc. I would say that the piano solo is a musical form which really does not interest me. I have always loved and played the piano, but my piano compositions are perhaps too facile; they are to be sure, well written for the instrument, which is one reason a number of great pianists have performed them. But they do not represent my truest feelings. I know only too well that I will never write a "Gaspard de la Nuit" by Ravel or a "Seventh Sonata" by Prokofieff.
>
> Where I really feel there is originality is in the piano accompaniments to my songs. This is because of the challenge that is present when I must express in musical terms the feeling and meaning of the poem.[17]

"The feeling and meaning of the poem"! Poetry was to inspire Poulenc to some of his finest compositions, and in the judgment of many, his greatest music is to be found in his songs.

In 1919, while he was on military duty at Pont-sur-Seine, the bookseller Adrienne Monnier, a friend of Linassier, sent Poulenc a copy of Guillaume Apollinaire's "Le Bestiaire." Poulenc had known these poems before, but this was a new edition illustrated by Raoul Dufay. They fired Poulenc's imagination. Some he memorized, and twelve he set to music. After showing them to Auric, he took his advice and allowed only six to be published, instructing that they were to be sung without interruption. Thus poet and composer joined in an inspired understanding which would result in some of Poulenc's greatest songs. These songs were the first of 146 which were published during his lifetime, many of them settings of Apollinaire texts.

It was during this time that Poulenc was identified with the "Groupe des Six." Though his piano works had attracted attention, he was most admired for his songs, and even though they showed the spirit, the melody, the small-scale dimensions which were a hallmark of "Les Six," Poulenc did not adhere to the general style which is attributed to these composers. Even though he was involved in the one project in which "Les Six" collaborated, *Les Mariés de la Tour Eiffel* of Cocteau, Poulenc pursued his own way. He felt that Ravel's counseling had been right—he needed further training. And he did not turn for such training to Satie, or to "Les Six," but to Charles Koechlin, the pedagogue and composer, who put him to work on four-part harmonizations of Bach chorale-melodies.

Poulenc saw Koechlin twice a week for the three years beginning in 1921 in what was to be his last formal training.[18] Koechlin did not "allow himself to be bound by the conventions of the schools. . . . having anticipated all the 'isms' and 'alities' before they became fashionable . . . he has seen the 'new music' catch up with him but never pass him."

> His attitude may be explained by the fact that he regards classical harmony as the basis of all composition, unlike the Schola which placed the greater emphasis on counterpoint. He is insistent that the basic technique be mastered before the student attempts to write "free" harmony or counterpoint. In this way he guards his students against those extremist tendencies which often become evident too early in their careers and have no technical foundation.[19]

Much has been written about "Les Six" and it is certainly true that Poulenc's identification with this group was beneficial to him. It is also true that the six musicians were allied more by friendship than by artistic inclination. They enjoyed each other and the comradeship inspired them. Their famous Saturday nights at music halls and circuses influenced them as creative artists. The sophisticated and disciplined talents of the clowns and circus performers of that era, and the music, charged with the new vitality of American jazz and the bistro songs, were in contrast to the music of the Parisian opera and theater. The wild rhythms and the new harmonies were in sharp opposition to what was being taught at the Conservatoire or the Schola Cantorum. These colors and contours found their way into the music of Ravel and Stravinsky as well as into that of "Les Six."

Although Poulenc did not study with Arnold Schoenberg, he did hold him in great esteem and, with Milhaud, he went to Vienna to visit him. The "Groupe des Six" had sent a "Greeting to Arnold Schoenberg" in 1918, while World War I was being fought, saluting him as a great composer and teacher. When the war ended, Poulenc and Milhaud left for Vienna with Marya Freund, who had given the first French performance of *Pierrot Lunaire* of Schoenberg. While in Vienna, at the request of Alma Mahler, they gave two performances of this work, one in French, one in German—one conducted by Schoenberg and sung by Erika Wagner and the other conducted by Milhaud. Of this performance, Milhaud wrote:

> It was a most exciting experience; Schönberg's conducting brought out the dramatic qualities of his work, making it harsher, wilder, more intense; my reading on the other hand, emphasized the music's sensuous qualities, all the sweetness, subtlety, and translucency of it. Erika Wagner spoke the German words in a strident tone, with less respect for the notes as written than Marya Freund who, if anything, erred on the side of observing them too closely. I realized on that occasion that the problem of recitative was insoluble.
>
> He invited us to call on him at Mödling, in the neighborhood of Vienna. We spent a wonderful afternoon together. At his request I played my second suite. Francis [Poulenc] played his Promenades for the piano which he had just completed.[20]

The "Sprechstimme" of *Pierrot Lunaire* and the use of the recitative technique in Poulenc's song style have much in common, in effect, if not in execution. Poulenc's admiration for and visit to Arnold Schoenberg invites speculation as to his influence.

One other trip with Milhaud broadened Poulenc's horizons. They went to Italy and hoped to give a concert at Santa Cecilia in Rome. But their reputations as members of "Les Six" prevented this and they had to settle for private hearings. No songs were written during this trip to Italy.

The next significant event in Poulenc's life was to lead him to another musical triumph, but it cost him his friendship with Satie. It was his commission from Diaghilev to write a ballet with Jean Cocteau which would in form follow classic ballet dances. The choreography was by Nijinsky and it was titled *Les Biches*. First performed at the Théâtre de Monte-Carlo on January 6, 1924, and in Paris the following May, it was a resounding success. However, Louis Laloy, the French critic who was carrying on a vendetta against Satie, began to praise both Poulenc and Auric at the expense of Satie. It was a disaster for Poulenc's relationship with Satie, who never made his peace with Poulenc.

After the tremendous success of *Les Biches*, his discharge from the army, and the eroding of the inner relationships of the "Groupe des Six," Poulenc began to compose works in various forms and for a variety of instruments. His song production increased as well, but it was not until 1931, when he again turned to Apollinaire for his texts, that his songs became inspired. In the same year, he set the poetry of Max Jacob for the first time. This Jewish mystic was to die in a Nazi concentration camp at Drancy, France, on March 5, 1944. Poulenc found another kindred spirit in this writer. Besides the poems of 1931, he set a secular cantata of Jacob's the following year—*Le Bal Masqué*. In 1935 he turned again to Jacob for the Parisian songs "Joueur de bugle" and "Vous n'écrivez plus?"

The same year, Francis Poulenc began his most productive song writing. It was the year of the first songs to poems of Eluard and the year that he established the partnership with the great French baritone Pierre Bernac. Poulenc has said that he learned the art of song writing by accompanying Bernac in works of Schubert, Schumann, Fauré, Debussy, and Ravel. The songs of this period will be dealt with in detail in the course of this study, but it should be stated that 86 of Poulenc's 146 songs were created from 1935 until the summer of 1956, and only a single song and one song cycle were written in his later life. Pierre Bernac told John Gruen in 1959 that Poulenc had entirely given up writing songs. In an interview in 1960, the composer himself told John Gruen that Bernac's contention was true, that if he continued to write songs he would only be repeating himself:

I am too old, besides Apollinaire, Eluard and Jacob are all dead. . . . I was an intimate friend of all three . . . and, somehow I understood their poetry extremely well. I was able to read between the lines of their poems; I was able to express all that was left unsaid in musical terms. Today, poets do not write in a manner that inspire me to song. I once told the young

French composer Boulez that I was too old for René Char and that he was too young for Eluard. But aside from all that, I have written well over 100 songs and to write more would be to force myself in a direction to which I really have nothing further to say.[21]

True to these words, there is but one addition to his list of songs after the last in 1958. This was written in 1960, when he set seven poems in a group of songs called *La courte paille*. The poet is Maurice Carême.

During the Second World War, Poulenc again served in an antiaircraft battery until the French army was demobilized in 1940. Then he returned to Paris, continuing to compose during France's dark years.

In 1945, for the first time a concert at the Salle Gaveau in Paris paid tribute to Poulenc as a great song composer. Suzanne Balguerie and Pierre Bernac collaborated with the composer at the piano in a concert devoted only to Poulenc's songs.

During the writing of his opera *Dialogues des Carmélites*, from 1953 until its completion and first performance in January, 1957, Poulenc endured the greatest personal crisis of his life. His depression was so immense that he did not expect ever to finish the opera, and his health was almost broken.

Two other works were completed before his death, *La Voix humaine*, a one-act opera premiered in 1959, and the *Gloria* for Soprano, Chorus, and Orchestra, which bears a close relationship to the style of his *Stabat Mater*. Poulenc heard the premiere in Boston in 1961.

Francis Poulenc died in Paris on January 30, 1963, of a heart attack. "His individuality was at once declared in the earliest of his works and gradually a world of his own has been marked out and described."[22]

Notes

1. Pierre Aubry (ed.), *Les Plus Anciens Monuments de la musique française*, Mélanges de musicologie critique, IV (repr. of Paris, 1905 ed.; New York: Broude Brothers, 1969), Pl. I.

2. James Husst Hall, *The Art Song* (Norman, Okla.: University of Oklahoma Press, 1953), 139.

3. Henri Hell, *Francis Poulenc*, tr. Edward Lockspeiser (London: John Calder, 1959), 87.

4. Pierre Bernac, *The Interpretation of French Song* (New York: Praeger Publishers, Inc., 1970), 269.

5. Martin Cooper, *French Music From the Death of Berlioz to the Death of Fauré* (London: Oxford University Press, 1951), 194.

6. Warren Kent Werner, "The Harmonic Style of Francis Poulenc" (Ph.D. dissertation, University of Iowa, 1966), 24.

7. Bernac, *Interpretation of French Song*, xiv.

8. Hell, *Francis Poulenc*, 13–14.

9. Norman Demuth, *Musical Trends in the 20th Century*, 70.

10. Darius Milhaud, *Notes Without Music* (New York: Alfred A. Knopf, 1953), 96, 97.

11. Vera Rašín, "'Les Six' and Jean Cocteau," *Music and Letters*, XXXVIII/2 (April, 1957), 167.

12. John Gruen, "Poulenc," *Musical America*, LXXX/5 (April, 1960), 6–7.

13. *Ibid.*, 26.

14. Allen Hughes, "Francis Poulenc, 1899–1963," *Musical America*, LXXXIII (February, 1963), 20.

15. Hell, *Francis Poulenc*, 2.

16. *Ibid.*, 9.

17. Gruen, "Poulenc," 26.

18. Hughes, "Francis Poulenc," 20.

19. Demuth, *Musical Trends in the 20th Century*, 18–19.

20. Milhaud, *Notes Without Music*, 139–40.

21. Gruen, "Poulenc," 7, 26.

22. Hell, *Francis Poulenc*, 87.

II Text & Music

"One must translate into music not merely the literal meaning of words but also everything that is written between the lines, if one is not to betray the poetry." [1]

Francis Poulenc

Poulenc found in poetry the exhilarating force of inspiration. It was a passion with him, as was his love of the human voice. "J'aime la voix humaine," he said. [2]

One of the most extraordinary facets of Poulenc's approach to song was his unerring integrity toward the poem. He constantly tried to preserve the form as well as the spirit of the poet's intentions. His ear for the timbre of the human voice and his striving for the aural sensitivity of verse won for him the respect and friendship of contemporary poets. His intimacy with these literary friends gave him an even keener insight of and appreciation for their work.

Three poets will be bound to Poulenc as long as French songs are sung—Guillaume Apollinaire, Paul Eluard, and Max Jacob. Poulenc was their Orphée. The majority of his mélodies are to poems of these three men, though the list of those who inspired him contains the spectrum of French poetry of the first half of the twentieth century: Jean Cocteau, Jean Moréas, Louise de Vilmorin, Colette, Maurice Fombeure, Louis Aragon, Raymond Radiquet, Robert Desnos, Henry Malherbe, and Maurice Carême. Other songs were set to sixteenth-century texts by Pierre Ronsard and to one poem by Charles d'Orléans; the *Chansons Gaillardes* are anonymous verses from the seventeenth century. Also, Poulenc contributed one *Vocalise.* Eight Polish poems and French verses of the Spaniard Federico Garcia-Lorca were also set. But the poets who were his personal friends were the ones to whom Poulenc felt the greatest kinship; to Apollinaire, Eluard, and Jacob went the best of his genius.

Apollinaire was thirty-eight years old at his death in 1918, the year after he and Poulenc had met. This was the time when Poulenc published Apollinaire's *Le Bestiaire*, his first songs for voice and piano. Apollinaire, standing between the Symbolists and the Surrealists, had been a tremendous influence on the modern literary movement in France, leaving a heritage of poetry and critical writings that would determine French letters in the twentieth century. Poulenc was then only eighteen years old, beginning a career that would make him one of the most significant composers of his nation and a man who would bring the poetry of contemporary Frenchmen into the concert halls of the world.

In order to understand Poulenc's approach to mélodie, it is well to start where Poulenc did, with the poetry and the poets:

I find myself able to compose music only to poetry with which I feel total contact, a contact transcending mere admiration. . . . I have never claimed to achieve this musical resolution of poetic problems by means of intelligence. The voices of the heart and instinct are far more reliable. This quality I felt for the first time when I encountered the poems of Guillaume Apollinaire. That was in 1912, when I was 13. Instantly, I fell in love with Apollinaire's poetry.[3]

Guillaume Apollinaire, born in Rome in 1880, was christened Wilhelm-Apollinaris de Kostrowitsky, his surname being that of his mother, Angelica de Kostrowitsky, a Polish lady who enjoyed a free lifestyle and bore two illegitimate sons, Guillaume and Albert. Flamboyantly, Apollinaire for years claimed to be the son of a high prelate in the Catholic church, but his father was probably Francesco Flugi d'Aspermont, an officer in the Italian army.

The two brothers lived different lives after attending Catholic schools in France. His mother left Guillaume entirely on his own at eighteen when he went to work in a Paris bank. However, he spent his free time in the cafés and made friends with Picasso, Max Jacob, and Marie Laurencin, who were also to play their part in Poulenc's musical life. During this period, he changed his name to Guillaume Apollinaire and began to earn his living as a critic and poet, "writing articles, stories, translations, theses for students, introductions to deluxe editions of erotic literature, children's books, and columns in the daily newspapers."[4] He also wrote some poems using the name Louise Lalanne.

His bizarre life in Paris attracted notoriety. When a friend stole the Mona Lisa from the Louvre, the police believed this crime might be connected with him, and Apollinaire was arrested and jailed before the thief was caught. Friendship with Picasso, Braque, and Gris led him to write "Les Peintres Cubistes," in which he explained the new movement. His poems "Le Bestiaire" and "Alcools" and his book "L'Anti-tradition Futuriste" established him as the voice of the avant-garde, and it was at the height of his success that France entered the war in 1913. Apollinaire, an Italian citizen, was safe from conscription, but he took French citizenship, enlisted in the army, saw action, and was wounded while fighting in the trenches. Returning to Paris a war hero, he wrote "Calligrammes" and a surrealist drama, "Les Mamelles de Tirésias," later set to music by Poulenc. He married in 1918, after an adventurous love life which included an affair with the painter Marie Laurencin. He and his wife, Jacqueline Kolb, enjoyed only a brief happiness, as Apollinaire died in the year of his marriage due to a flu epidemic which swept Paris.

In Apollinaire's poetry one finds free forms and traditional rhyming verse. He strove for clarity both in style and content of his poems so often directed to the human condition of joy, love, sorrow, and the quicksilver of time. Irony and tragedy, lyric joy and beauty exist together in his poetry, much of it descriptive of Parisian life. As to Apollinaire's poetic style:

> What appears to characterize all his verse, both the lyrics and the free verse, is an integrity of line, a desire to make each line a partially self-sufficient unit which does not depend too

greatly upon the succeeding line. This integrity of line extends to an integrity of stanza and of the poem itself, and thus we arrive at the secret of his composition at its most successful. Each line is like a brick in a wall and is an essential part of the structure; yet each is still clearly defined and distinguishable within its setting. His lines are highly articulated syntactically and rhythmically. This composition testifies to an intrinsic logic in Apollinaire's vision, to a desire to avoid unnecessary complexities, and to a keen feeling for unity in his verse. . . . As evidence of the soundness of this construction, there is the fact of the total lack of punctuation from all of Apollinaire's verse beginning with "Alcools."[5]

Poulenc set thirty-five poems of Apollinaire. Three contrasting poems—"La Carpe," the final song from *Le Bestiaire*, and "Voyage à Paris" from *Banalités*—may illustrate Poulenc's unerring understanding of text setting which complements and enhances the poetry rather than distorting it.

Le Bestiaire ou Cortège d'Orphée (*The Book of Beasts or Procession of Orpheus*) contains six of Apollinaire's twelve quatrains, the music of the other six being destroyed by Poulenc on the advice of Georges Auric. Unlike the medieval animals, they were not allegorical but living beasts. "The Carp" is the climactic song in Poulenc's cycle. The fish is found abundantly in ponds and streams all over Europe. The carp was thought to enjoy longevity denied other creatures, folklore attributing to it a life span of at least a hundred years. Apollinaire writes:

In your fish-pond in your pools
carp how long you live
is it that death has forgotten you
fish of melancholy.

   This poem gave both Apollinaire and Poulenc an opportunity to comment upon the human condition symbolically reflected in the seemingly endless life of this creature which, due to the forgetfulness of death, continues its endless slow swimming locked into the boundaries of the man-made pool. This neglect of death created the image of "fish of melancholy," a timeless quality characteristic of Apollinaire poetry. The lack of punctuation, the short, succinct, rhyming couplets of four lines, the imagery of the carp as timeless, and the acceptance of circumstance shared by all men are present, and Poulenc successfully conveys them to the ear. Immediately the mood is set—"Très triste-Très lent," cautions Poulenc, and "Les 2 pédales." The two-bar introduction to be played "sans nuances" conveys the impression of the slowly swimming fish, the two pedals employed assure a liquid overlapping sonority, and the steady, repeated E flat all work together to establish the image. The ceaseless motion between basic chords (tonic and dominant) and the reiterated E flat in the right hand form an endless pedal point. The chords have no thirds except when rarely supplied in the melody. Again, this deliberate obscuring of fixed major or minor tonality renders an uncertainty which enhances the character of "neglect" in the symbolism of the poem.

The voice sings in double pianissimo throughout, entering on the syncopated beat, a slight displacement in time, poetically and musically expressed, yet the continuous swimming of the fish is uninterrupted as the pianist continues to play the exact rhythmic patterns and alternating repetitious figures until the final sustained pedaled chord "laisser vibrer." The voice enters on the established note of E flat not to disturb this undulating monotony and continues in recitative throughout the short piece. What melodic movement is present confines itself to the third and an octave leap.

The use of the descending leap is poetically valid as a call on the word "Carpes." At the word "Poissons" (fish) the third is ascending and less urgent as a more muted call. The octave leap is reserved for the climax of the song, with A flat dramatizing the key word of the song, "Mélancolie." The total effect of the musical setting captures perfectly the spirit of the poetry.

In contrast, the doggerel verse used in "Voyage à Paris" from "Banalités" has a totally different flavor. Here, the famous dance-hall style, for which Poulenc has been damned and praised, is present in all its charm. The accompaniment has an almost mechanical-piano-roll sound with its rhythmic accent on the downbeat of the café waltz. It captures what Apollinaire called his "Poèmes conversations."

In composing verse he seems to have had two methods between which his work is polarized and they explain to some extent the aural effects of his poetry. One method was to write while humming a tune to whose rhythm he could fit words. It seems to have been almost a mechanical means of keeping track of the meter, for Apollinaire was not musical. The other method was that of combining almost at random the odd sentences and phrases that occurred to him or that he overheard. "Poèmes conversations" he called these last . . . several of the lyric poems in his work seem to be almost pure sound, whose exploration of vowel qualities, of alliteration, and of rime is simple and pleasing. One of his very early poems, "Voyage à Paris," is of such a nature.[6]

Poulenc admonishes the pianist and singer "Très allant" and "Gai" as he launches into ten measures of introduction, halting suddenly at measure 7, a café music cliché. Then, three more bars of the introduction before the singer enters; and the uneven stanza lines say:

> Ah what a charming ride
> To leave a gloomy countryside
> > For Paris
> > Lovely Paris
> > Which long ago
> Love must have beautified
> Ah what a charming ride
> To leave a gloomy countryside
> > For Paris

This poem is one of Apollinaire's essays in aural amusement, written with an ear to alliteration as well as in exploitation of rhyme. For Poulenc, this poem is more than a contest with doggerel. He has taken poetic liberty in the rearrangement of some lines as repeated parts of the poem. The original reads:

> Ah la charmante chose
> Quitter un pays morose
> > Pour Paris
> > Paris joli
> > Qu'un jour
> Dut créer l'Amour
> Ah la charmante chose
> Quitter un pays morose
> > Pour Paris.

To these lines, Poulenc added:

> Paris joli
> Ah Quitter un pays morose
> Charmante chose

This addition forms the content of the third section of this song. The composer seldom tampered with the order of verses in the poetry he set to music. Apparently he felt with doggerel it was acceptable.

In order to emphasize further the rhyme, Poulenc places the ending syllable of many words on the downbeat of this waltz song. The cabaret style is maintained in the use of several other devices—the constant repetition of tonic and dominant in the bass, the primitive concept of the lyrical melody, and the limited range of the melody.

Vocal indications to the singer, such as "Très lié," "Avec charme," "Très naturel," "Très aimable," as well as the instruction to falsetto on the high G, which is in the normal range for the singer, reinforce the concept. This falsetto instruction would not be necessary for a true chanteur since it is a natural effect in cabaret singing.

The introduction of the "blue" note in measure 40 with the flatted seventh supporting the word "Paris" adds more flavor.

Poulenc's ending for this song shows a sensibility for the text line. The last "Chose" is given an A flat dissonance over an incomplete seventh chord before returning to the tonic. This gives interesting color, dramatizes the ending, and leads to a linear progression for the piano coda. It is interesting to note that Poulenc was a great admirer and friend of Maurice Chevalier, who was singing in Paris at this time (1940). In this song one is reminded of the vocal style of that great entertainer.

Apollinaire explored many avenues of sensuous expression in both his creative efforts as a poet and in his probing as a critic. He believed that poetry should be read aloud and that its visual aspects were as much a part of its effect as its content. The placement of words on a page, the typeface used, punctuation, all add to the total sensation. The visual aspect of poetry, the attempt to make a poem an object of an aesthetic experience, was already pursued by the French poet Panard, who lived in the eighteenth century, and by the Englishman George Herbert. They relied upon the ideogram, an object described by the arrangement of types. Apollinaire manipulated twenty-eight of his poems in a visual arrangement which was conceived as a part of the total concept. These he called "Calligrammes." Roger Shattuck refers to them as "a plastic arrangement of words in three different fashions to represent the objects being described; to represent a total conception of the universe; and to express a movement of thought within the poem."[7] A great poem might not benefit from this kind of visual treatment. But the spatial manipulation adds drama and perspective to the written word, and probably enhances a less profound poem.

Poulenc set seven songs from the "Calligrammes" in 1948. Each was dedicated to a friend of the past, and the cycle is a farewell to Apollinaire, as Poulenc felt his inspiration from the poet was diminishing. "Il Pleut" (Example 1) is typical of these poems.

How does Poulenc attempt to transfer the poem and its visual concept into sound? He effectively makes one hear the rain in the accompaniment. And it is interesting to observe that one can see as well as feel the raindrops while *looking* at the piano accompaniment. There is no relief from the sixteenth-note figures until the last seven measures when triplets appear below the ever-pounding sixteenths. Here, too, appears the descending figure in the right hand of the piano as the drops fall one by one. The use of the pedal, indicated in explicit instructions, and the change of meter to keep the pulse constant while accommodating the words allow no letup in momentum.

The imagery of the poem is formed by Poulenc into a poetic declamation in melody, though not recitative. He punctuates and underscores with musical stress, gives rapid impetus to some words, slowing others so as to prolong them and make the

IL PLEUT

Example 1

Text & Music

Il pleut des voix de femmes comme si elles étaient mortes même dans le souvenir

c'est vous aussi qu'il pleut merveilleuses rencontres de ma vie ô gouttelettes

et ces nuages cabrés se prennent à hennir tout un univers de villes auriculaires

écoute s'il pleut tandis que le regret et le dédain pleurent une ancienne musique

écoute tomber les liens qui te retiennent en haut et en bas

listener aware of the meaning. The singer becomes the reader of the poetry, adding the color of the voice to that of the music to achieve the poet's intent. Said Poulenc of Apollinaire: "I always have in my ears the sound of his voice so special, half-ironic, half melancholy."[8] Poulenc translated "the sound of his voice" into music, capturing the spirit of the poet in his songs. He probed more deeply than the words. He looked into the man.

After his studies with Koechlin, Poulenc often turned to Georges Auric for criticism of his work. Auric felt that Poulenc had little understanding of early French poetry, and Poulenc agreed that he was disappointed with his setting of *Cinq Poèmes de Ronsard*. Auric urged Poulenc to consider the French contemporary poets. In 1935, Poulenc turned to Paul Eluard, setting five of his poems. Two years later he composed *Tel Jour Telle Nuit*, the great song cycle which ranks with *Le Bestiaire* in popularity with recitalists.

Paul Eluard was born Eugène Grindel, the son of a bookkeeper. He was one of those poets whom Poulenc met in his youthful days when he was browsing the bookstores with Raymonde Linassier. Eluard contracted tuberculosis in his teens and spent almost two years in Switzerland in a hospital. There he became a voracious reader, discovering the French poets. When he returned to France in 1914, he joined the army, serving in the infantry on the front lines where he was gassed and suffered severe lung damage.

After the war, Eluard was attracted to the Dadaist movement and became acquainted with Tzara, Aragon, and Breton. Dadaism was an artistic protest movement based on deliberate irrationality that sought to break the traditional laws of organization. Eluard later moved away from Dadaism because of its negativeness. His friendship with Jean Paulhan, who sponsored the work of so many young poets, was also a significant event in his development. The young poets and the painters Ernst, Chirico, and Picasso banded together in another movement later called surrealism. This was in 1924. It proclaimed that nothing less than total liberty in all human activities was undeniable. Surrealism strives to produce fantastic or incongruous imagery by means of unnatural juxtaposition and combinations of elements.

One of the more exotic declarations of the surrealists dealt with the relation of the sexes. A clarification of the place of women in literature as partners of men both spiritually and physically was one of their contributions. Eluard went even further and proclaimed that through love man would paradoxically escape the world yet know the world best. To him love was a total physical and mystical union.

In his love poetry Eluard refused to separate the external world of the senses from the inner world of the soul and the mind. His style is precise, direct yet subtle. He addresses himself to basic conditions of man: poverty, suffering, and joy in the events of his daily life. Love for woman transcended personal relationship and became a universal experience. "Dismissing reason and intelligence as tools of doubtful poetic unity, Eluard announces in Donner à Voir: 'I do not invent the words. But I invent objects, beings, events and my senses are capable of perceiving them. . . . My reason refuses denial of the testimony of my senses. The object of my desires is always real, tangible.'"[9] This is almost a paraphrase of Poulenc's declared approach to composition, noted in the opening lines of this chapter. It is little wonder that the composer found inspiration in Eluard's poetry.

Eluard was deeply involved in the French Resistance during World War II and was pursued relentlessly by the Gestapo. He remained in France, fighting in the underground and writing resistance poetry which was circulated by word of mouth or by the underground press. He became a militant Communist, as were his friends Picasso and Aragon. Eluard died in 1952.

In "Tel Jour Telle Nuit" Poulenc found the poems for his great song cycle. The nine songs, each contrasting in musical style and mood, are among his finest. The poet, overwhelmed by Poulenc's incisive understanding, wrote to the composer after the first performance:

> I hardly listened to myself Francis
> Francis through you I now hear myself
> On the whitest of roads
> Through a vast landscape
> Soaked in light
> Night has now no roots
> Shade is behind mirrors
> Francis we dream of distance
> Like a child with an endless game

In the starlit country
Giving in return youth.[10]

Tel Jour Telle Nuit is a true cycle. In many instances of song sets, one mélodie may be logically selected for a program, but these are interdependent, each bound to the other.

"Bonne Journée" ("A Good Day") opens the cycle. Imagery conveys subconscious reflections on normal events in such phrases as "and women fleeting by whose eyes formed for me a hedge of honor" and "his shadow changed into a mouse and fled into the gutter." A serenity, despite the intrusion of dark thoughts, marks the poetry. How does Poulenc deal with these various elements?

Lilting duplets doubled at the octave for the first eight measures give the song the overall joyful character. The duplet figure continues without letup until the final coda. Spontaneously, without introduction, and over this figure, the song begins: "A good day, I have again seen whom I do not forget." The phrase "whom I do not forget" is built on the same motive as the opening phrase, only extended, which binds the two thoughts, that it is a good day *because* I have again seen the one I do not forget. The composer abandons the octave doubling but keeps the duplets moving for "and women fleeting by whose eyes formed for me a hedge of honor." With this line a rising melody is associated, building tension to the word "honor." In these few measures the song moves from the major tonality through the minor, returns to the major on the word "eyes" and continues through "formed for me a hedge of honor." In this way, the imagery of the poem is colored, sustaining the lucid movement through the bright and dark of major-minor. The same words, "a good day," open the second stanza. Then follows "I have seen my friends without care." For these words the same motive with a change in rhythm is used. The construction reads: "The men were light in weight, one who passed by, his shadow changed into a mouse fled into the gutter." For this metaphor, Poulenc employs a counter-melody in the piano. Different words begin the third verse: "I have seen the wide, great sky, the beautiful aspect of those deprived of all." Again the same motive is used, this time embellished chromatically, placing even greater tension on the opening phrase. At the beginning of the last stanza, "A good day" returns, followed by the poetic clause "which began the melancholy." Here the pace slows down (half notes) but still stays with the motive. As there is a return to the major tonality, the word "melancholy" loses its ominous meaning somewhat. However, beneath the words "dark under green trees, but which suddenly drenched with dawn, invaded my heart" two chords appear simultaneously, one emphasizing minor tonality. On the last words of the poem, "without surprise," the brighter major mood is prevailing. The duplets are abandoned for the first time in favor of a chordal ending, which ascends to the upper register of the piano to confirm the joyous mood. Thus subtle musical devices support the imagery and the joyful calm is secure. The composer will return to some of these devices, including the use of the main motive, in the final song to achieve unity for the whole cycle.

The second song, "Un Ruine Coquille Vide" ("A Ruin an Empty Shell"), is set to a poem which builds atmosphere through surrealistic description of juxtaposition of opposites. Poulenc immediately indicates the mood by the direction "very calm and unreal" and prescribes both pedals to create an eerie sonority. In the piano introduction a bell-like tolling sounds, which continues subtly throughout the song. This creates a perfect atmosphere for the words: "A ruin an empty shell / weeps into its apron / the children who play around it / make less sound than flies." Bernac says, "I personally imagine that the apron into which the ruin cries is suggested by heavy masses of ivy tumbling down the old walls."[11] The music moves in the slow pace of the poem. The harmonic rhythm is slow, the melodic line moves in even quarter and eighth notes, with little change in contour. Poulenc seemed to have in mind a total concept throughout the song for overall effect, rather than characterizing specific detail. "The ruin goes groping to seek its cows in the meadow / I have seen the day I see that / without shame. It is midnight like an arrow / in a heart within reach / of the sprightly nocturnal glimmerings / which gainsay sleep." The only contrast appears at the end. Poulenc writes a recitative for the words "which gainsay," and over the sounding persistent bell, the voice descends an octave and rises a fifth for the word "sleep." No change in dynamics is indicated, as the bell sounds to the end.

"The Brow Like a Lost Flag" ("Le Front Comme un Drapeau Perdu") is a "mélodie of transition and contrast." Coming after the atmospheric "Ruin," "it begins in violence and ends in a strange peacefulness."[12] With an upbeat in the voice, the song thrusts forward as indicated, "très animé." The opening voice lines are doubled in the piano for added vigor. The mixolydian mode provides color for the words: "The brow like a lost flag / I drag you when I am alone / through the cold streets / the dark rooms crying in misery." Poulenc abruptly changes the violent mood as the poem suddenly becomes reflective: "I do not want to let them go / your clear and complex hands / born in the enclosed mirror of my own." The accompaniment becomes more transparent, reduced to two lines, played in octaves. Later the voice line is doubled, not at the same time, as anticipation and delay create a pulsating feeling. More motion is added to the accompaniment, but it remains simple, still in two lines for the declaration "all the rest is perfect / all the rest is even more useless / than is life." The next phrase, "Hollow the earth beneath your shadow," is set off in a two-measure phrase followed by a short two-measure interlude. It prepares the erotic ending of the poem with static chords and an undulating bass line for the words "A sheet of water reaching the breasts / whereinto drown oneself." The final three words, "like a stone," utilize the same static chords, this time dramatized by the bass line playing faster octaves, the final picardy third saved for this moment of poetic ecstasy.

"A Gypsy Wagon Roofed With Tiles . . . " suggests to Hell "an evocation recalling some lugubrious recitative of Mussorgsky."[13] Certainly there is a foreboding and sinister quality in this short poem. An almost snarling recitative is written in short bursts, punctuated by rests in the voice line with even, hammered chords accentuating the text. "A gypsy wagon . . . covered with tiles . . . the horse dead . . . a child master." This poetic description promotes a darker mood achieved with full chordal support, marked by harsh dissonance for "Thinking his brow blue with hatred" (no pause) "of two breasts beating upon him." The pedal point holds as the chordal movement continues steady, relentlessly signifying how "this melodrama tears away from us the sanity of the heart." A simple two-note embellishment on the final word, "heart," captures the mood of futility.

Bernac and Hell refer to "Riding Full Tilt" as a transitory song which psychologically prepares the listener for the one to follow. "Riding full tilt you whose phantom / prances at night on a violin / come to reign in the woods" are lines delivered over a galloping prestissimo accompaniment. An even more dense piano part, still keeping the blistering prestissimo, supports "the lashing of the tempest / seek their path by way of you / you are not of those / whose desires one imagines." A jagged vocal line builds the climax: "Come drink a kiss here / surrender to the fire which drives you to despair."

"Scanty grass / wild / appeared in the snow / it was health / my mouth marvelled," so begins the next poem. A simple chordal setting accentuates the tranquillity of this lyrical description heralding the first new grass of spring and the tender awakening of a first sensual encounter which then transforms innocence into womanhood. Only once does the tonality change in the entire song, breaking the mood for the words "at the savour of pure air it had / it was withered." A repetition of the first three lines of the poetry above an only slightly altered accompaniment follows. The simplicity of the music is equal to the serene lines of the poetry.

"I Long Only to Love You" is a perfect example of Eluard's concept of the totality of love. Poulenc, recognizing the explicitness of the verses, wrote a through-composed song. Driving rhythm and frequent harmonic changes animate the words. The scalewise melody, interrupted by chromaticism, completes the musical palette. "I long only to love you / a storm fills the valley / a fish the river" is the text of the first lyric verse. Not until the words "I have formed you to the pattern" is there a hint of key change. Instead, reiterated triplets determine the mood of serenity. The word "my" is accentuated by embellishment in the next phrase: "I have formed you to the pattern of my solitude." A modulation brings another color for the last phrases: "the whole world to hide in / days and nights to understand one another." The same tonality prevails in the last verse: "to see nothing more in your eyes." A new key and chromatic alterations increase color and tension for "but what I think of you." The accompaniment then thins out before the repeated chordal agitation for the ending lines: "and of days and nights ordered by your eyelids."

The thrusting start of the next song jolts the senses. It builds up in speed and intensity, thrashing the words in bitter, short, musical phrases, punctuated by rests. "Image of fiery wild forcefulness . . . black hair . . . wherein the gold flows toward the south." These lines of violent emotion are supported by stabbing repeated chords beneath the recitative. Octaves syncopated and accented in the left hand, over which the right hand plays an agitated figure, are a perfect complement of the voice line. "On corrupt nights . . . engulfed gold tainted star . . . in bed never shared . . . ." Silence extended by a fermata follows. This hold prepares the listener for a pentatonic figure in the piano, melting into two contrasting lines, one ostinato, giving exotic color to the words "to the veins of the temples / as to the tips of the breasts / life denies itself / no one can blind the eyes." Weight is added to the accompaniment, leaving the voice to intone in recitative "drink their brilliance or their tears." To further support the word painting, an ostinato figure of moving notes, using larger note values, slows the text: "the blood above them triumphs for itself alone." A sudden broken chord-cluster and a chromatic ostinato supply color and tension: "untractable unbounded / useless / the health holds a prison." A dramatic upward leap on the word "prison" states the climax.

Poulenc said, "It is only calmness that can give a love poem its intensity."[14] "We Have Made Night," the final song of this cycle, is a sublime love poem of Eluard. It is related to the first mélodie by recurring motives, duple figures, mood, key, and piano postlude. Beginning with the same motive as the first song, the cycle concludes:

> . . . I hold your hand I watch over you
> I sustain you with all my strength
> I engrave on a rock the star of your strength
> deep furrows where the goodness of your body will germinate
> I repeat to myself your secret voice your public voice
> I laugh still at the haughty woman whom you treat like a beggar
> at the fools whom you respect the simple folk in whom you immerse yourself.

In the piano postlude, at the change of meter, the final measures of the first song return, unifying the cycle musically and poetically: "A good day I have again seen whom I do not forget, whom I shall never forget" and "We have made night / I hold your hand I watch over you." Blue notes in the final chord are a symbolistic ornament, a last touch of imagery, an impressionistic element, leaving much to the imagination as was the intent of this surrealistic poet.

Poulenc felt Eluard was "unique in contemporary French literature as a lyricist and poet of love." He held Eluard "responsible for having bestowed real lyricism on my music. Every composer eventually discovers what he considers to be his own source of greatness. I have found it in the poetry of Paul Eluard." [15]

Destiny was not kind to Max Jacob, another source of Poulenc's inspiration. Born in 1876, Jacob was reared in Britanny, becoming a poet of Montmartre, actor, vagabond, clown, mystic, and martyr. Always extremely poor, working at any job which would provide a living, Jacob pursued his life without bitterness. He was a friend of those who were to achieve lasting fame—Apollinaire, Juan Gris, Francis Garco, and Picasso. The latter shared living quarters and what little money he had with him. It was Picasso who acted as Jacob's godfather when the poet was finally accepted into the Catholic faith after six years of soul-searching.

In 1921 a move to Saint Benoît-sur-Loire, near a Benedictine church, provided seclusion for work and an atmosphere that enabled Jacob to dedicate himself to his poetry and to his new-found religious ideals.

When the Germans occupied France nearly twenty years later, Jacob was forced to wear the Yellow Star signifying his Jewish birth. He was arrested in February of 1944, taken to Drancy, and killed by the Gestapo on March 5, 1944, at the age of 68, despite the desperate efforts of his friends to save his life.

Jacob's poetry is a combination of parody, satire, and improvisation; his creative talents are perhaps most akin to those of Satie. Jacob influenced many of the poets of the middle twentieth century. Some visited him, others wrote and sent their work to him for criticism.

In the cantata *Le Bal Masqué*, written in 1932, Poulenc truly captured the spirit of Jacob's poetry, the two men seeing as one in discerning the nature of Parisian Bohemia as they lived and understood it.

A year earlier, Poulenc had set *Cinq Poèmes* by Jacob, containing "Chanson bre-tonne," "Le cimetière," "La petite servante," "Berceuse," and "Souric et Mouric." Two of these exemplify Jacob's rakish style.

"La petite servante" ("The little servant") begins "Preserve for us thunder / thunder runs like a bird / it is God who guides him." Agitating octave figures in thirty-second notes imitate thunder. At the words "It is God who guides him," the intervals widen, the figure continues unabated through the next thought, "Blessed to be the damage." A hurrying descending chord sequence figure heralds "If it is the devil / who leads us / get us out of here." The motion ceases suddenly. There is silence in the vocal line. A new accompaniment—um-pah . . . um-pah—at the meter change fits to Jacob's jocular phrases, "Preserve our pimples / the pests in the fields / If it is for my penance." At the word "penance" chromatic sixteenth notes sneak in. At the word "God" a thickening of texture is evident. "If it is the devil / who leads / Get us out of here" is in the text. But the accompaniment is not the same as before, only dry chords punctuated with rests. "Goiter, get out of your bag / from my throat and head." Repeated sixteenth notes characterize "St. Vitus Dance." The repeat of the thought of devil and God is musically illustrated by a wide leap in the vocal line and a beginning descent in the piano, terminated with a measure of rest lengthened by a fermata. The last section of the song brings a complete change in texture, meter, and motion. The accompaniment eludes all tonality. It is a parody on a prayer: "Make it possible that I grow / and give me a husband / who will not drink too much / who will not beat me all night." The end is sudden and whimsical.

"Souric et Mouric" is a nonsense poem. The beginning, "White rat and black mouse," is unaccompanied except for one chord. At the next phrase, "that came into my cupboard / to teach the spider to make a web on the loom / to make a linen sheet," wide leaps are used in the piano, and a delayed one measure may depict the spinning. Bolero rhythm suddenly follows: "Send to Paris, Quimper or Nantes / to sell it / put pennies away / you will buy a field." The music keeps up with the sudden change of style. "Apples and many cows and a bull / to make bulls" show static color chords. "Sing, red apples / and when the night comes / we will hear frogs calling / black birds magpies / listen all the day you will learn to sing." Here a bird call introduces the final cantabile section which is sustained until the end. Poulenc has enlivened the descriptive aspects of Jacob's poetry, underlining the buffoonery.

"C," so significant in its meaning to all Frenchmen, was performed at almost every concert shared with Pierre Bernac. It was either listed on the programs or requested by the audience before the artists were allowed to leave the hall. This writer was present when Bernac, explaining its significance to the American audience, said it was often sung in the presence of the Germans during the war as an act of defiance and patriotism.

The occupation of their country by the Nazi army was an intolerable time for the French. The poem "C," written by Louis Aragon, "recalls the dark days of 1940, and the tragic exodus of the French population as it fled before the invading forces. In a tone of extreme melancholy, the poet speaks of crossing the river Loire at a place called Les Ponts de Cé, and describes all that this journey through the confusion of a forsaken France brings to his mind."[16]

Louis Aragon was a founder of Dadaism and surrealism and, after a visit to Russia in 1931, became an avid Communist. This political persuasion caused a break with André Breton and the surrealist group. In a series of books, Aragon began to attack fascism. When the war broke out, he fought until the army was disbanded and then became a leader of the underground movement. His poetry, anti-German, inflammatory and largely autobiographical, was secretly circulated throughout France. After the war he assumed his duties as director of *Le Soir*, a leftist newspaper.

In French the letter "C" is pronounced "se" as in sedilla. Every line of this poem ends with that syllable, regardless of the word. Written in four verses and an added couplet, there is a melancholy mood of acceptance. The tonality is minor and the harmonic rhythm slow, melodic contrast masking the continuous repetition of "Cé." Sequences, reserved for the endings of the stanzas, give an insistence to the text of the last verse: "the Loire carries my thoughts away / with the overturned cars / and unloaded weapons / and not yet dried tears." Nowhere in Poulenc's songs does he achieve more poignancy than in the final couplet: "Oh my France, oh my forsaken France, I have crossed the bridges of Cé." Sudden halts on the words "forsaken" and, finally, "bridges of Cé" release an overwhelming expression of repressed emotions.

Louise de Vilmorin was another favorite of Poulenc. "I have found in her poetry a sensitive impertinence, a wantonness and gluttony. Few others have moved me as much as she." [17] "Violon" from *Fiançailles pour rire* is typical of her verse.

> Enamoured couple with misplaced accents
> the violin and player please me.
> Ah! I love these long extended wailings
> on the cord of uneasiness.
> In chords on cords of the hanged
> at the hour when laws are silent
> the heart, in the shape of a strawberry
> gives itself to love like an unknown fruit.

A double-stop figure in the right hand of the accompaniment imitates the café violinist. The left hand plays a typical cabaret dance tune. Over this, the vocal line is sung in portamentos, parlando, and "exaggerated" café effects. Poulenc dedicated these songs to Vilmorin when she was imprisoned in Hungary in 1939.

Pierre Bernac said that Poulenc had little respect for Jean Moréas. The composer validated this by writing in his *Journal de mes Mélodies*: "I am constantly astonished at ever having thought of writing these songs. . . . The fact is, that I loathe these poems of Moréas and I chose them for this very reason, namely, I thought they deserved to be torn to shreds."[18] This reverse integrity is most evident in "Air Champêtre" ("Pastoral Song"). The fourth line should read "Perdu sous la mousse à moitié" ("Half hidden beneath the moss"). "Mousse" is dissected in parody: "Perdu sous la mou, sous la mousse" ("Half hidden beneath the mo, beneath the moss").

In "Air Vif" ("Lively Song"), the fifth line of the first verse reads "Hélas! et sur leur tête" ("Alas! and above their head"). In this song, "Hélas!" repeats four times, giving a ridiculous twist to the verse: "The riches of the orchard / and the festive garden / flowers of fields / of wood / burst forth with delight / Alas! Alas! Alas! Alas! and above their head / the wind's voice is rising."

Despite his disdain, Poulenc's melodic gift never deserted him, even in times of disgust, and these songs have proven popular with audiences.

Other poets fared better. Jean Cocteau is represented by *Cocardes*, three popular songs of 1919 originally written for voice and small orchestra. "Enfant de Troupe"

("Child of the Troupe") is a circus poem in the disjointed style of Cocteau: "Caramel . . . bonbons . . . free game in satin . . . Hamburg . . . glass of beer . . . blue uniforms . . . trapeze . . . incense of death." Imitation of the calliope, trumpet fanfares, a march, brash music hall tunes are juxtaposed to complement the kaleidoscopic words. "Trapeze . . . incense of death."

Jean Cocteau discovered the Cirque Médrano with Picasso, Apollinaire, and Jacob. As with Picasso, circus performers influenced his poetry, novels, plays, ballets, and movies. "His role was to hide poetry under the object."[19]

Chansons Villageoises (Village Songs), written by Maurice Fombeure, were composed originally for baritone and orchestra. They are "recreations of a primitive peasant spirit in music . . . though folk songs of a kind . . . the music is only loosely tied to the text. . . . Poulenc admits having been influenced by the cast of vocal phrase used by Maurice Chevalier."[20] Impressionistic color tones, polychords, and chromaticism enrich the harmony of this cycle.

Raymond Radiguet, poet and companion of Poulenc's youth, died very young. "Paul et Virginie," a conversational poem dedicated to the author, preserves the dialogue by contrasting melodic motives and harmonic color.

"Epitaphe," by the distinguished critic Henry Malherbe, "written in memory of the composer's friend Raymonde Linassier, was inspired by the sight of a noble building of the period of Louis XIII."[21]

Three songs contributed by Federico Garcia-Lorca, the great Spanish poet, were translated into French by Félix Gattegno. Perhaps this is why a perfect union of text and music is not achieved. Musically their Spanish flavor is maintained in the strong rhythm, reminiscent of Ravel, in hand-crossing, chromaticism, and impressionistic oscillation of chords.

Huit Chansons Polonaises, written in 1934, are Polish patriotic songs of the insurrection of November 29, 1831, when the youth of that beleaguered country rose against the occupying troops of Russia, Germany, and Austria. The melodies are traditional Polish tunes (Poulenc composed the accompaniments), with verses in Polish authored anonymously or by poets who fought in this short-lived liberation movement. They are the only songs of Poulenc in a language other than French, though a French translation is supplied. Six of them are mazurkas, two polkas. The particular rhythmic accents and style of these Polish dance forms, carefully observed, authenticates them as Polish, specifically intended by the composer to be sung in the native language.

Chansons Gaillardes is a setting of seventeenth-century anonymous verses. Their wit celebrates the pleasures of the flesh. They are constructed with the rhythmic drive, syncopation, and narrow range of bawdy melodic character.

Verses by Charles d'Orléans and Ronsard represent historical material, and among Poulenc's contemporaries are found Colette, Laurence de Beylié, and Maurice Carême as sources of poetic inspiration.

It is fitting to end this chapter with one of Poulenc's last songs, "Dernier Poème." The poet, Robert Desnos, was another tragic figure of World War II. Arrested by the Gestapo in 1944, Desnos was interned at concentration camps in Fresnes, Compiègne, Buchenwald, and Auschwitz. Liberated by the Russians in 1945, he died of starvation and typhoid in a rehabilitation camp in Terezine, Czechoslovakia.

Desnos enjoyed a stream of constant inspiration, acknowledged by Eluard and other poets. Breaking with the surrealist movement, he continued to seek the unusual and bizarre. His poetry is often erotic and full of imagery. Desnos wrote for many literary magazines, participating in underground publications of the French Resistance, especially *Les Editions de Minuit*.

"Dernier Poème" is very transparent and retains a simple accompaniment throughout. Considerable use of pedal is combined with low tessitura. Chromatic alterations mist over and soften the dynamic level for these last words, which Desnos wrote to his wife:

> I dreamed so much of you
> I walked so much, I talked so much,
> Loved so much your shadow
> That nothing more is left for me of you;
> Except to be a shadow in the shadows
> To be a hundred times more shadow than shadow.
> To be a shadow who will come and yet come again
> Into the sunshine of your life.

Notes

1. Robert Jacobson, Record Notes, *Songs of Poulenc*, Gerard Souzay and Dalton Baldwin, RCA Victor LSC–3018.
2. *Ibid.*
3. *Ibid.*
4. Roger Shattuck (trans.), *Selected Writings of Guillaume Apollinaire* (New York: New Directions, 1971), 7.
5. *Ibid.*, 26.
6. *Ibid.*, 21.
7. *Ibid.*, 19.
8. Anita Earle, Record Notes, *Francis Poulenc 1899–1963*, Souzay-Baldwin, Phillips Records PHS 900–148.
9. J. H. Matthews, *Surrealist Poetry in France* (Syracuse: Syracuse University Press, 1969), 107.
10. Hell, *Francis Poulenc*, 53.
11. Bernac, *Interpretation of French Song*, 293.
12. *Ibid.*, 294.
13. Hell, *Francis Poulenc*, 51.
14. Bernac, *Interpretation of French Song*, 298.
15. Jacobson, Record Notes, *Songs of Poulenc*.
16. Bernac, *Interpretation of French Song*, 276.
17. William B. Ober, Record Notes, *Poulenc Songs*, Westminster Records WST 17105.
18. Hell, *Francis Poulenc*, 34.
19. Wallace Fowlie, *Mid-Century French Poets* (New York: Twayne Publishers, 1955), 119.
20. Hell, *Francis Poulenc*, 65.
21. *Ibid.*, 38.

III Melody

Poulenc's strict adherence to the character of the French language gives each song a melodic uniqueness explicitly devised to meet specific and implied demands of the poetry. Pierre Bernac, who observed the creative progress in Poulenc's song writing, states, "He had an exceptional feeling for French declamatory style and his melodic gift, which was the very essence of his music, inspired him to find the appropriate musical line to heighten the expression of the literary phrase."[1]

In the following discussion, first the general characteristics of Poulenc's melody—its shape, motion, and direction—will be dealt with, followed by its specific attributes. Mostly, the composer uses the diatonic idiom, though some chromaticism is to be found. The melodic motives are organized in various ways, constructed in phrases, phrase-groups, and periods. These may be in regular symmetry, which is often found in the folklike and cabaret songs, or in segments of irregular length, sometimes even in declamatory, recitativelike sections where subdivisions are impossible.

Melodic Shape

Regarding the songs in general, several basic principles can be discussed: the curves of the lines; changes of direction; and the position and nature of the climax points.

A rather typical example of Poulenc's melodic preferences is in "Une herbe pauvre" from *Tel Jour Telle Nuit*. It consists of several segments divided by rests or long notes which are alternately ascending or descending. In the first segment (measures 1–3), ascending and then gently descending curves occur with the climax on E near the beginning (Example 2). The second segment has about the same shape, only that the

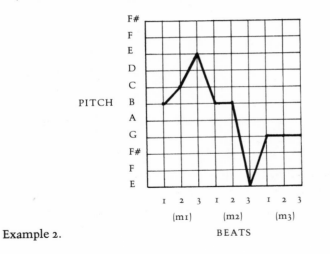

Example 2.

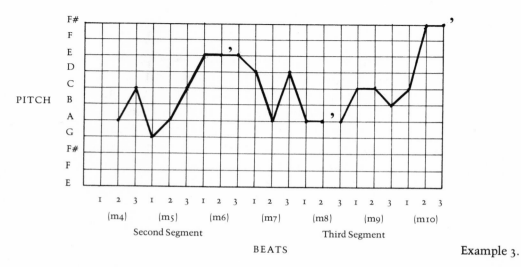

Example 3.

climax is at the end (measure 6). The line continues on the same note and leads downward (third segment). An ascending part follows, which leads to a final climax on F sharp, one tone higher (Example 3).

In the middle of the song, the first two bars (11–13) show wider curves, but later motion is slowed down and no climax is found (Example 4).

The last part of the song shows curves similar to the first section, but in higher tessitura, as the climax here is on B. The final segment drops back again to E, which was

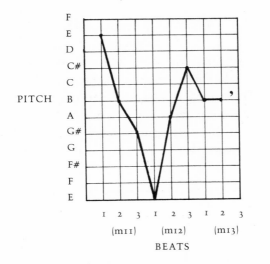

PITCH

BEATS

Example 4.

the climax in the beginning. A diagram of all sections reveals a deliberate position of the high points (E, F, G, E).

The alternation of segments in different directions can be found in most of the songs; the first phrases usually lead upward to a climax, the next downward to a low point.

"Chansons de la fille frivole" from *Chansons Villageoises* is characteristic of interval leaps without much curval motion; therefore, no special climaxes or anticlimaxes are found. This song, which shows melodic chromaticism, will be mentioned later.

Gentle curves are abandoned in several songs. For instance, in "Nuage" from *Deux Mélodies 1956*, only the top notes, extracted from every segment, suggest a small downward motion. The characteristics of the melody are the large interval fifth leaps which are persistent and may express the anxiety of the poetry (Example 5).

In the beginning of this song (measures 5–6), melodic curves are minimal because of the small intervals (Example 6). From bar 7 on, the intervals are somewhat larger and

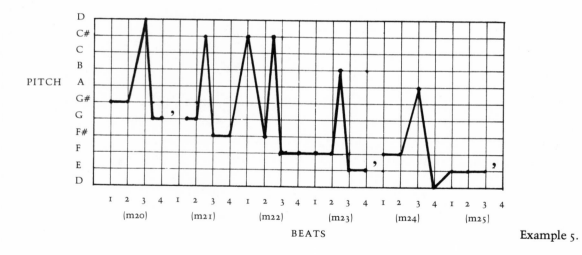

Example 5.

Example 6. "Nuage" from *Deux Mélodies 1956*, measures 5–6. Copyright 1956 by Eschig, Paris. Used by permission.

the tessitura lower. Still there is no definite melodic trend, the lines approaching declamatory character. This change is found throughout the song.

In "L'Offrande," from the seventeenth-century texts of *Chansons Gaillardes*, short segments in small range alternate with others which have wider intervals (Example 7). Due to the melodic independence of the sections, a single curve for the entire song cannot be established.

The trend toward climaxes and low points, melodic tension and relaxation is found in miniature in almost every phrase, a point of arrival or retreat from that point. This principle is valid, also, for the songs as a whole concerning their high and low points in pitch and dynamics.

Example 7. "L'Offrande" from *Chansons Gaillardes*, measures 6, 9, 12, 17, 21. Copyright 1926 by Heugel, Paris. Used by permission.

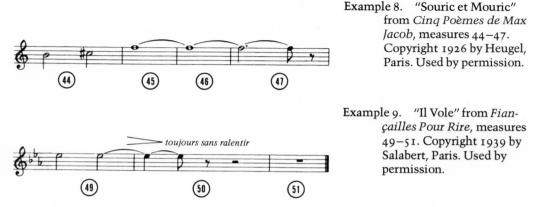

Example 8. "Souric et Mouric" from *Cinq Poèmes de Max Jacob*, measures 44–47. Copyright 1926 by Heugel, Paris. Used by permission.

Example 9. "Il Vole" from *Fiançailles Pour Rire*, measures 49–51. Copyright 1939 by Salabert, Paris. Used by permission.

toujours sans ralentir

"Chanson Bretonne" from *Cinq Poèmes de Max Jacob* reserves the highest note of the song, E, only for a moment on the final syllable on the word "voix." Except for an E flat in bar 5, the tessitura of the entire song is much lower. In "Souric et Mouric" from the same set, the highest note, F, is sustained for three bars as climax (Example 8).

The effect of a final climax can be achieved by a long sustained high, soft note, which may not be the highest in the song, as, for instance, in "Il Vole" from *Fiançailles Pour Rire* of Louise Vilmorin. The E flat is held for two bars at the end, though the voice has risen to B flat repeatedly in the middle of the song (Example 9). Also, in "La belle Jeunesse" from *Chansons Gaillardes*, the final fortissimo D is sustained for six bars, not

Poulenc's Songs   60

Example 10.   "Air Vif" from *Airs Chantés*, measures 72–76. Copyright 1926–27 by Salabert, Paris. Used by permission.

the highest note, which is F. The feeling of the climax is achieved by duration, not by pitch.

A final note sustained, like the D held for four bars at the end of "Air Vif" from *Airs Chantés*, is not felt as a climax as it is preceded by a virtuosic coloratura which reaches a climactic high A flat (Example 10). In the coloratura itself, the characteristic waving lines can be observed.

"C," the French Resistance song, owes its fame as one of Poulenc's finest compositions to many factors, not the least of which is the writing of the climax. Here climax is achieved by a combination of high pitch and low dynamic. It is interesting that in this apostrophe, "O ma France, ô ma délaissée" ("Oh, my abandoned France"), the crescendo is suddenly interrupted, and the highest intensity is reached in pianissimo (Example 11). To emphasize the dramatic character of this song, Poulenc changes the dynamics and tempo in every bar.

Proceeding to the specific character of Poulenc's melodies, it has already been

Example 11. "C" from *Deux Poèmes*, measures 37–41. Copyright 1943 by Salabert, Paris. Used by permission.

stated that he prefers diatonicism, either scalewise or triadic, to chromaticism, which plays only a minor melodic role.

A typical example of scalewise movement as melody is "La belle jeunesse," measures 1–6. It is interesting that the scalewise motion is employed in different directions as well as in different rhythms (Example 12). Similar scale segments occur throughout the song. Here the character of the voice line is almost instrumental.

The beginning of the voice part of "Les Gars Polonais" from *Huit Chansons Polonaises* is purely triadic as in the original folk melodies (Example 13). The melody type is sustained for the greater part of the song. However, in the latter half, we find diatonic scale segments.

Example 12. "La belle jeunesse" from *Chansons Gaillardes*, measures 5–10. Copyright 1926 by Heugel, Paris. Used by permission.

Example 13. "Les Gars Polonais"
        from *Huit Chansons*
        Polonaises, measures 1–4.
        Copyright 1934 by Salabert,
        Paris. Used by permission.

One of the comparatively few examples of melodic chromaticism is found in the beginning of "Chansons de la fille frivole" from *Chansons Villageoises*, repeated in bar 2. It consists of a descending chromatic scale. Bars 21 and 22 contain ascending chromatic scales (Example 14). These segments appear several times throughout the song.

Melodic Organization

Poulenc prefers, in general, short melodic motives. Longer unbroken lines appear less frequently. The short musical thoughts have mostly definite melodic contour; however, units based entirely on rhythm without much melodic content are frequent.

Example 14. "Chansons de la fille
        frivole" from *Chansons
        Villageoises*, measures 1–2
        and 21–22. Copyright 1942
        by Eschig, Paris. Used by
        permission.

63   **Melody**

Example 15. "La Couronne" from *Huit Chansons Polonaises*, measures 1–8. Copyright 1934 by Salabert, Paris. Used by permission.

Regularly organized melodies are the rule, but sometimes the units are uneven due to the meter of the poetry. The set of eight Polish songs are the best examples for simplicity and regularity, since they are taken from the idiom, but we find a more sophisticated means in these pieces which are akin to the rhythm of modern cabaret and even jazz music.

The first of the Polish folk songs, "La Couronne," demonstrates this regularity clearly. Even the piano introduction, which has mazurka rhythm with its very wide melodic leaps, is quite regular. The eight bars start with two connected two-bar groups

Example 16. "La Couronne," measures 9–16.

and with the three-fold repetition of the inverted head-motive of the first bar, followed by a cadence in the tonic (Example 15).

Interesting, too, are the subtle relationships between bars 2 and 4 through the identity of chromatic progressions.

The following eight bars of the song consist of four two-bar units which are, except for their ending, almost identical. The first four bars are repeated exactly (Example 16).

Similar organization is found in the other folksongs, for example in the third. Slight deviation is found in the second song, where only the second two-bar group is repeated.

The songs associated with Poulenc's Parisian life often touch the coarse vernacular. "Voyage à Paris" from *Banalités* is a waltz with a typical "Eingang" (tonic-dominant) for six bars. The waltz rhythm is sustained throughout the song (Example 17).

The melody consists of sixteen bars, the first four exactly repeated, the last (also sung twice) containing only cadential long notes. Characteristic are the rests after every four bars. The words "Paris," "L'amour," and "Jolie" in this song are emphasized, partly by slurs and indications of falsetto characteristic of the chanteur. The composer stresses the mood by such indications as "avec charm," "aimable," etc.

65 **Melody**

Example 17. "Voyage à Paris" from *Banalités*, measures 1–16. Copyright 1940 by Eschig, Paris. Used by permission.

In the accompaniment of the song "Violon" from *Fiançailles Pour Rire*, a very slow waltz rhythm, the pseudogypsy double stops and glissando of the café violinist are imitated. Here the organization of the introduction is 4-plus-1 bars for the first part, and two one-bar groups for the end. The whole unit has only seven bars (Example 18). But

Example 18. "Violon" from *Fiançailles Pour Rire*, measures 1–7. Copyright 1939 by Salabert, Paris. Used by permission.

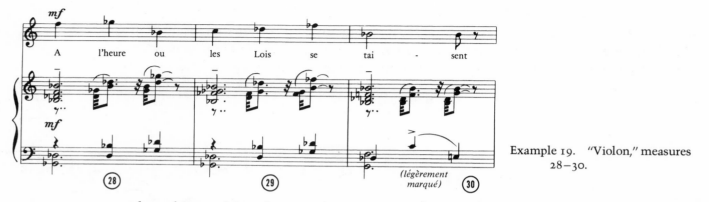

Example 19. "Violon," measures 28–30.

when the vocal line begins, the regularity of 2-plus-2-plus-4 is reestablished and kept except for one three-bar group (Example 19).

Nonfolklike songs often show the typical two-bar group organization, as in "Marc Chagall" from *Le Travail du Peintre*. However, here the structure of the different segments varies. The introduction of twelve bars consists of two melodic two-bar motives, then of a four-bar unit that is different but melodically related to the first group. The last four bars contain only chords, descending triadically. The following vocal melody is added to the skeleton of the introductory twelve bars, which here are played by the piano (Example 20).

The beginning of "Chanson Bretonne," previously mentioned in this chapter, opens with the familiar two-bar units. In the center of the song, however, four bars lack

Example 20.   "Marc Chagall" from *Le Travail du Peintre*, measures 1–13. Copyright 1956 by Eschig, Paris. Used by permission.

Example 21. "Chanson Bretonne" from *Cinq Poèmes de Max Jacob*, measures 19–22. Copyright 1931 by Salabert, Paris. Used by permission.

melodic contour. There are rhythmic repetitions of one tone (Example 21). Four bars more of melodic line follow, the last note of which is extended for two bars. The third part of the song returns to the motive of the beginning in augmentation, so that two-bar groups extend into four.

"La Grâce Exilée" from *Calligrammes* exemplifies a mixture between regular and irregular bar groups. In the first part, the repetition of the head-motive is exact, while the second group is one bar longer, four against five. During the last two bars of this group, the piano plays the pickup head-motive *on* the beat of two three-bar groups (Example 22). At the finish, a three-bar group appears and the note values are longer without changing the basic rhythm.

One bar is repeated in the beginning of the song "Main dominée par le coeur" of Paul Eluard. The following two bars of the first unit are different, but the stress is always on the third beat. In bars 5 and 6, rhythmic accentuation is weaker. To bar 6 another bar is added, plus two bars in longer note values. So, the total unit has 1-plus-1-plus-2 (same stress); 1-plus-2-plus-2 (Example 23). In the second part of this song, one- and two-bar groups of the same shape alternate.

Example 22. "La Grâce Exilée" from *Calligrammes*, measures 1–3 and 9–10. Copyright 1948 by Heugel, Paris. Used by permission.

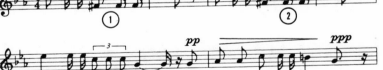

Example 23. "Main dominée par le coeur," measures 1–7. Copyright 1947 by Salabert, Paris. Used by permission.

71 **Melody**

The poetry of "Il Pleut" from *Calligrammes*, with its changing accents, necessitates irregular grouping, though the number of bars is symmetrical. The first melodic unit comprises four bars, but the beats are differently subdivided, 3-plus-4, later 4-plus-3; together fourteen beats (Example 24). The following phrase, five bars, is also subdivided into two units in different organization. In the beginning we find 2-times-3 beats, the same as at the end. In the middle is one four-beat unit; together sixteen beats (Example 25). The next section increases the number of beats to twenty-one (2-times-3, 2-times-4, plus an additional one bar with 3 beats and one with 4). The last part contains five bars of four beats each (total twenty). On the whole, the increasing of the number of beats in every unit (14-16-20-21) represents the composer's formal approach to the poem.

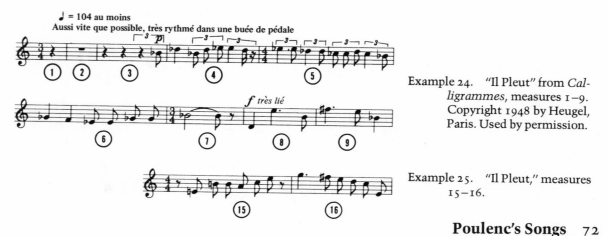

Example 24. "Il Pleut" from *Calligrammes*, measures 1–9. Copyright 1948 by Heugel, Paris. Used by permission.

Example 25. "Il Pleut," measures 15–16.

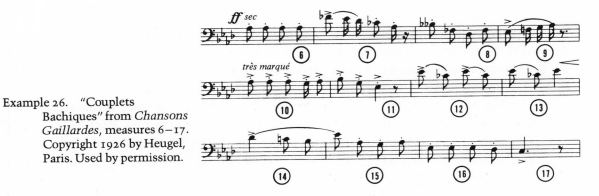

Example 26. "Couplets Bachiques" from *Chansons Gaillardes*, measures 6–17. Copyright 1926 by Heugel, Paris. Used by permission.

The song "Il Vole," already cited in Example 9, page 60, because of its repetition of the beginning, is noticeable by the change of melody type. The first part is in short note values, almost declamatory. The second part has long lyric lines, some in sequences. The end of the song returns to the rhythm and character of the beginning.

The voice line of "Couplets Bachiques" from *Chansons Gaillardes* represents a transition between melodic style and declamation. The rhythm is steady, strong, and dancelike. Also, the bar groups are symmetrical. However, as the note values are short and repeated tones are numerous, the impression of animated declamation is created (Example 26).

Pure declamation is rarely found in the body of Poulenc's songs. It appears in the shape of recitativelike sections, or irregular interjections between more melodic parts. The latter is the case in "Il la prend dans ses bras" from *Cinq Poèmes de Paul Eluard*,

73   **Melody**

where, after two melodic bars, free interpretation of the text occurs, almost spoken. After a fermata, the melodic line is resumed in bar 7. In the second part of the song, declamation is inserted again, this time in a question ("Qui donc à crié?") without piano accompaniment (Example 27).

In "Le Cimetiére" from *Cinq Poémes de Max Jacob*, the whole middle part (ten bars) is recitativelike, framed by the lyric first and last sections (Example 28). With the change of melodic style, the key is different also (A flat versus C).

An initial sparsely accompanied recitative is found in the beginning of "Souric et Mouric" from the same group (Example 29).

"Un roulotte couverte en tuile" from *Tel Jour Telle Nuit* varies the note values to

Example 27.   "Il la prend dans ses bras" from *Cinq Poèmes de Paul Eluard*, measures 1–6 and 7–8; 17–18. Copyright 1935 by Durand, Paris. Used by permission.

Example 28. "Le Cimetière" from
Cinq Poèmes de Max Jacob,
measures 14–17. Copyright
1931 by Salabert, Paris.
Used by permission.

Example 29. "Souric et Mouric"
from *Cinq Poèmes de Max
Jacob*, measures 1–2.
Copyright 1931 by Salabert,
Paris. Used by permission.

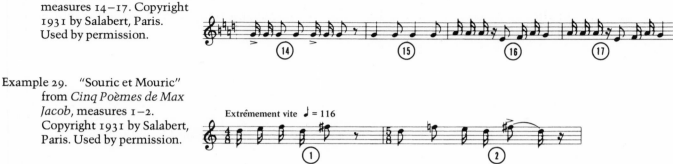

meet word stress, while rests are used for both dramatic silence and punctuation. Accent marks are put above some notes, often on unaccented beats. Meter changes indicate speed, and slow the tempo. Triplets, fermatas, and breath marks also assist careful word delivery. The accompaniment consists of steady chromatic chords in quarter notes marked "très lent et sinistre."

After exploration of Poulenc's melodic style in its different facets, it becomes evident that he always successfully "found the proper prosody when setting words."[2] Whether his texts came from the seventeenth century or the twentieth, Poulenc met their specific requirements and projected their essence to the audience, carefully ob-

75   **Melody**

serving the spirit of the French language in structure and meaning. His inventive use of various melodic principles and chameleonlike ability to assume the color and character of the poem give to each of his songs a singular individuality. They represent an ideal marriage of word and tone.

Notes

1. Bernac, *Interpretation of French Song*, 269.   2. *Ibid.*, 5.

IV Harmony

There is no consistent harmonic style in Poulenc's music, because he uses indiscriminately material ranging from the most simple diatonic harmonies to the most complicated cluster chords. Nevertheless, the basis of his harmonic language is tonal, as the traditional harmonic devices of the classic and romantic eras predominate. Upon this foundation, Poulenc's aural imagination constructs twentieth-century sonorities, often masking harmonic conservativism with impressionistic devices.

Definite tonalities and key centers underscore the traditional approach. Pedal points, ostinatos, and clearly functional bass progressions establish tonal relations which may be colored by sporadic uses of extraneous harmonies. Instances of polytonality and simultaneous use of the major and minor modes are present.

In chord construction, tradition and innovation exist in close proximity. Tertian sonorities with predictable alterations alternate with a combination of fourths, impure octaves, chord mixtures, or free sound combinations.

Tertian harmony predominates. However, seventh chords often shed their traditional restrictions and the necessity of being prepared and/or resolved. They are treated as independent sound entities, supplying color options to the composer. Triads plus added seconds or fourths, seventh chords plus sixths or ninths or chords of higher order are not resolved, but used as units. Nonchordic tones appearing in Poulenc's harmony may also be classified according to tradition, but most of them are color tones, not explainable except by sound effect.

Functional chord-connections abound in progressions that gravitate toward the tonic through the subdominant and dominant regions. Progressions by mediant relationships are also common. Inherited from the impressionists is nonfunctional harmonic side-slipping or gliding. Juxtaposition of chords without connective devices is frequent.

Ambiguity prevails in cadence construction. Expected authentic, plagal, tritone, and half-closings are present, as are modal endings such as II-I or IV-V# in minor formulae (Phrygian), these often according to demands of the text. Most frequently, Poulenc prefers the authentic cadence, but in most of his punctuations color-tones enrich or even veil the tonality. Despite these additions, it is through the cadences that key centers are confirmed. No matter what harmonic wanderings take place before, the cadence assures tonal orientation, and here Poulenc's tonal harmonic style is established, though not always by traditional means. Even when there is no clear cadence feeling, a reiteration of chords, voice leading toward a final point or bass progressions will eventually set a key center for the ear.

True modulations are rare in Poulenc. Instead, the aforementioned shiftings of the tonal center for a measure or two or for a whole section are almost always linked to the exigencies of the text. Often abrupt changes are used for word-oriented aural shock. What often seems a modulation is only a short detour achieved by enharmonic spelling, use of ambiguous chords (diminished sevenths or similar chords), or temporary chromaticism to obscure the root feeling and vary the established harmonic texture, if only momentarily. A more strident effect is the juxtaposition of alien chords, an option Poulenc often elects. His aim is to keep an ever-shifting key center perilously constant. These tonal trips, though calculated, often give the impression of improvisation.

Nonharmonic tones are abundant in Poulenc's chords. They may be passing tones, appoggiaturas, suspensions, échappées, and cambiatas. Many are the result of contrapuntal convergence. Most of the apparent aggregates can thus be explained; true clusters are present, but rare. Specific examples of these general observations reveal the composer's rich harmonic vocabulary.

Pure Diatonic Chords, Pedal Points, and Ostinatos

The first song cycle establishes a strong key orientation never to diminish. *Le Bestiaire* begins with "Le Dromadaire." Its tonal center is, clearly, E, exactly expressed by the fourteen-measure repetition of E in the bass line, its reiteration becoming a firm pedal (Example 30). This tonality is undisturbed by the G sharp and C natural of the first chord, which represents a simultaneous major and minor above it. The effect is the impure octave of G-G sharp. In the second chord the subdominant A-C-E is introduced, again the A combined with A flat and E altered to E flat, a "neapolitan" effect. This con-

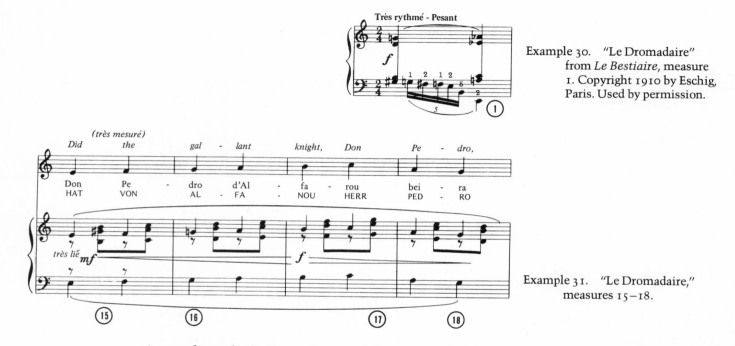

Example 30. "Le Dromadaire" from *Le Bestiaire*, measure 1. Copyright 1910 by Eschig, Paris. Used by permission.

Example 31. "Le Dromadaire," measures 15–18.

tinues through the second part of the song, where the tonality is again E. Later, faster harmonic rhythm occurs by harmonizing the diatonic scale degrees (Example 31). The final cadence is purely authentic in E (Example 32).

"Voyage à Paris" from *Banalités* uses the alternations of tonic and dominant, so

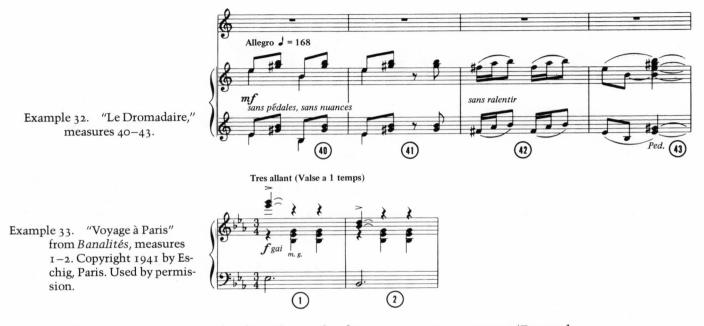

Example 32. "Le Dromadaire," measures 40–43.

Example 33. "Voyage à Paris" from *Banalités*, measures 1–2. Copyright 1941 by Eschig, Paris. Used by permission.

typical of Poulenc's adaptation of café style, in the first twenty-six measures (Example 33). This sequence of V-I in the bass reiterates the E-flat tonality, interrupted by chromatic descending six-four chords and color tones in the pseudo-Viennese waltz section (Example 34).

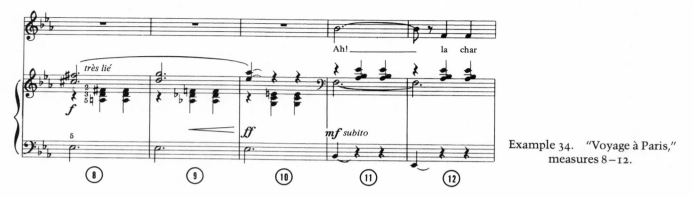

Example 34. "Voyage à Paris," measures 8–12.

An interesting harmonic device occurs in "La Sauterelle" from *Le Bestiaire*. The tonic is arrived at by sequence, II-V-I-IV (I). At the third beat of the first measure it already appears, but veiled. Then, it clearly appears at the first beat of the second measure (Example 35).

Example 35. "La Sauterelle" from *Le Bestiaire*, measures 1–2. Copyright 1920 by Eschig, Paris. Used by permission.

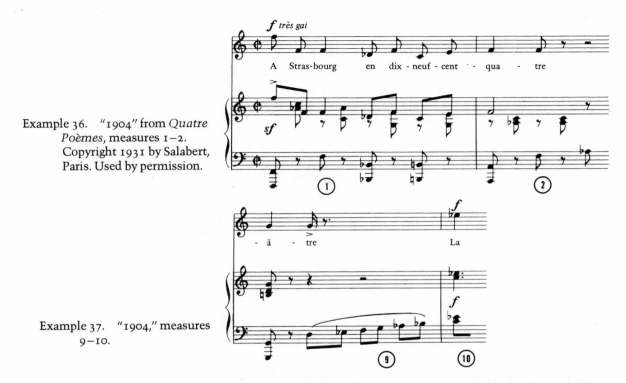

Example 36. "1904" from *Quatre Poèmes*, measures 1–2. Copyright 1931 by Salabert, Paris. Used by permission.

Example 37. "1904," measures 9–10.

Rarely does a song begin in one key and end in another. Short excursions into different keys usually return, in the final bars, to the key first established. Not so with "1904" from the set of *Quatre Poèmes* of Apollinaire. The first measures establish F minor with the I-IV-V-I progression (Example 36). Poulenc reaches the dominant C minor conventionally at measure 10 (Example 37), where he remains until measure 20, when suddenly A minor occurs (Mediant relationship) (Example 38). A typical harmonic sequence (chromatic descending bass) stops at B flat (and B sharp) and returns to C minor again. Ascending in sequence to D, the tonality changes. After rests, the following cadence is added: B flat^6, E$^6_4$, D^7 (with A flat instead of A), where the song ends. The bass note, D, remains as pedal through this cadence. The B flat in the voice part is nonharmonic, a color sound. The end, on G, contrasts with the beginning in F minor (Example 39).

The eleven-measure song "La Carpe" from *Le Bestiaire* is a perfect example of ostinato (A-flat minor plus V flat and IV). Designed in two-measure units, the ostinato repeats exactly throughout the piece below a changing melodic line. Timelessness and continuous predictable motion, which are dictated by the poetry, are achieved by this device (Example 40).

Example 38. "1904," measures 18–20.

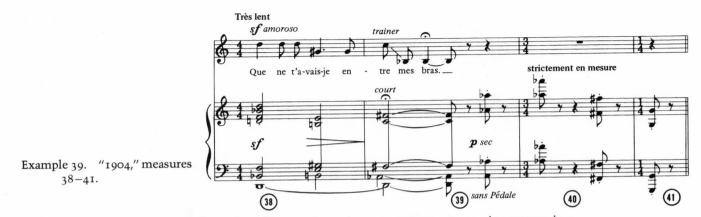

Example 39. "1904," measures 38–41.

Beginning in a major mode and ending on its minor counterpart, or vice versa, is a frequent occurrence. Therefore, naming a few songs as examples will suffice: "Chansons de l'Oranger Sec" from *Trois Chansons de Garcia-Lorca* (C minor-C major); "Figure de force brûlante et farouche" from *Tel Jour Telle Nuit* (D minor-D major); "Mon cadavre est doux comme un gant" from *Fiançailles Pour Rire* (E minor-E major); and "Aussi bien que les cigales" from *Calligrammes* (E major-E minor).

Example 40. "La Carpe" from *Le Bestiaire*, measures 1–2. Copyright 1910 by Eschig, Paris. Used by permission.

85 **Harmony**

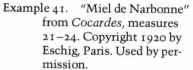

Example 41. "Miel de Narbonne" from *Cocardes*, measures 21–24. Copyright 1920 by Eschig, Paris. Used by permission.

Polytonality

The functional progression of I-V (D-A in D major) is used several times in "Miel de Narbonne" of *Cocardes*. However, in the upper voices the harmony of F-sharp minor, plus its dominant (C sharp), is implied. Thus, polytonality results (Example 41).

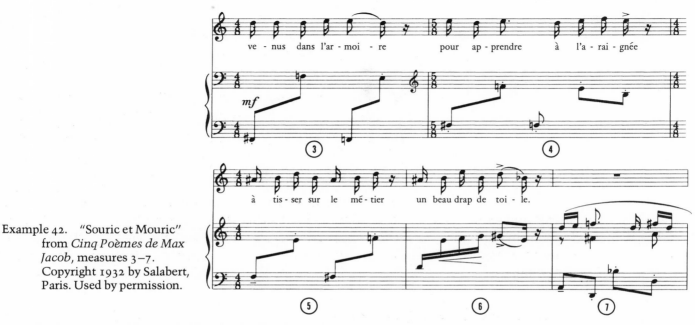

Example 42. "Souric et Mouric" from *Cinq Poèmes de Max Jacob*, measures 3–7. Copyright 1932 by Salabert, Paris. Used by permission.

Simultaneous Major-Minor and Impure Octaves

Alternating major and minor thirds, already noted in Example 30 (page 80), create impure octaves, characteristic for "Souric et Mouric" from *Cinq Poèmes de Max Jacob*. The tonal center is D (major/minor); F sharp versus F natural and F versus E provide a capricious exchange in keeping with the ambiguity of the poetry (Example 42).

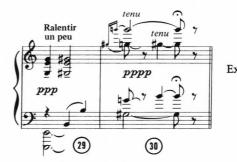

Example 43. "Vers le sud" from *Calligrammes*, measures 29–30. Copyright 1948 by Heugel, Paris. Used by permission.

Another striking example of the dissonance factor is in the use of impure octaves, major and minor at the same time. In the final cadence (measures 29–30) of "Vers le sud" from *Calligrammes*, the impure octave is derived from the use of both major and minor forms of the E triad, simultaneously. Marked pianissimo, it has a veiling effect (Example 43).

Alterations of Tertian Chords

Conventional progressions are sometimes veiled by chord alteration. The secondary dominant ninth chord (D-F sharp–A flat–C-E flat) in "Bonne Journée" shows a flatted fifth, but the cadence (measures 27–29) is clear, D^9-G^7-C (II^9_5-V^7-I) in C major (Example 44).

Example 44. "Bonne Journée" from *Tel Jour Telle Nuit,* measures 27–29. Copyright 1937 by Durand, Paris. Used by permission.

"Dernier Poème," one of Poulenc's last songs, relies upon the most basic device of diatonic tonality, I-V-I in E minor. Some of the harmonies in the middle can be explained as secondary dominants (Example 45).

Chord Mixtures or Free Sound Combinations

A ninth chord appears in the final cadence of "La Maîtresse Volage" from *Chansons Gaillardes* in B-flat major (measure 45), where it functions as a combination of the in-

89   **Harmony**

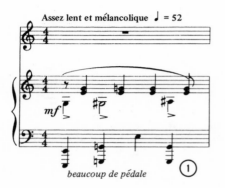

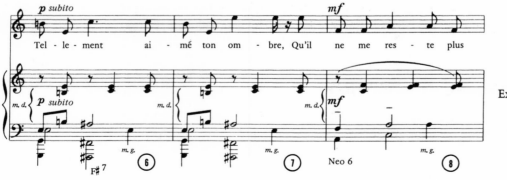

Example 45. "Dernier Poème," measures 1, 6–8. Copyright 1957 by Eschig, Paris. Used by permission.

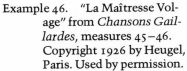

Example 46. "La Maîtresse Volage" from *Chansons Gaillardes*, measures 45–46. Copyright 1926 by Heugel, Paris. Used by permission.

complete minor dominant (F-A flat) and the G major triad (altered VI) which leaves the tonality open (Example 46).

Poulenc sometimes chooses to maintain an established tonality and at the same time superimpose upon it free and unrelated chordal elements. Such is the case in "Le Lac" from *Huit Chansons Polonaises*, measures 18–21, where the vocal line and the right hand of the accompaniment are clearly in E minor, while the left hand employs free sound combinations based upon the half-diminished seventh chord on C and the impure octave C-C sharp on C (Example 47).

Mediant Connections and Gliding Chords

Sometimes the preferred connection in romantic and later music is the mediant. "Tu vois le feu du soir" from *Miroirs Brûlants* yields this deviation from the more tra-

Example 47. "Le Lac" ("Jezioro") from *Huit Chansons Polonaises*, measures 18–21. Copyright 1934 by Salabert, Paris. Used by permission.

ditional fifth relationship, reinforcing in three measures a new melodic idea. The C-sharp minor tonality of the song is interrupted at measure 50 by a shift to C-sharp major (spelled enharmonically D flat) moving on to F minor. In measure 51, C minor moves to E minor/major, still in third relationship. Measure 52 is a contraction of the two preceding measures with exact harmonic repetition. A return to the C-sharp tonality is accomplished with two diminished seventh chords with roots in the third relationship. The C-sharp tonality anticipates the final cadence of the song at measure 59 after a two-measure excursion into C major (Example 48).

Gliding or side-slipping is an impressionistic device often used by Poulenc. Gliding chords move by step in parallel motion and can be both diatonic and chromatic,

Example 48. "Tu vois le feu du soir" from *Miroirs Brûlants*, measures 50–52. Copyright 1939 by Salabert, Paris. Used by permission.

though chromaticism is far more extensively employed. Chromatic side-slipping is employed in measures 27–31 of "Le Portrait." Here, the chords follow in descending chromatic motion (Example 49).

Color Chords and Pure Sound Effects

Harmonic tension is often created by color chords after simple diatonic triads. Measure 8 in "Le retour du sergent," the last song in *Chansons Villageoises*, shows this technique. One hears the F-sharp triad plus B and D. In the next chord D sharp is added to

Example 49. "Le Portrait," measures 27–31. Copyright 1939 by Deiss, Paris. Used by permission.

the same F-sharp triad. The bass progression F sharp-C sharp emphasizes the key. Immediately a repetition of the previous triads dispels the tension of color (Example 50).

Certain color chords are not reduceable to tertian types. A combination of fourths tends to mask the tonal centers which, however, are achieved by bass progressions and a most active voice line. "Le retour du sergent" uses this technique in its opening measures. The vocal line asserts the tonality of A minor in spite of the strong feeling of F major in the bass progression F-C. The chords in the piano show accumulated fourths and ninths (Example 51).

Less spectacular color chords appear in abundance in "Hôtel" from *Banalités*. The blissful, lazy mood of this poem is painted by the quiet legato tonic and submediant chords enhanced by the added second, ninth, and added sixth. In measure 2, B-flat^7 is preceded by an altered ninth chord plus added sixth (Example 52).

Example 50. "Le retour du sergent" from *Chansons Villageoises*, measures 6–8. Copyright 1943 by Eschig, Paris. Used by permission.

95 **Harmony**

Example 51. "Le retour du sergent," measures 1–2.

Example 52. "Hôtel" from *Banalités*, measures 1–2. Copyright 1941 by Eschig, Paris. Used by permission.

Cadences

As stated in the beginning of this chapter, Poulenc prefers the authentic cadences, but rarely are they simplistic statements—more probably a final flight of imagination. The

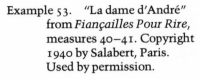

Example 53. "La dame d'André"
from *Fiançailles Pour Rire*,
measures 40–41. Copyright
1940 by Salabert, Paris.
Used by permission.

last cadence of "La dame d'André" from *Fiançailles Pour Rire* (measures 40–41) is V⁷-I in A (Picardy third). A pedal sustains the tonic chord; the minor dominant with an added second is sounded pianissimo above it, a pure sound effect (Example 53).

Groups of chords are sometimes used to extend the cadential feeling. This is Poulenc's choice in "La belle jeunesse" from *Chansons Gaillardes*. Concluding in D major with a V-I (measures 69–70), one measure follows (71) in which seemingly unrelated chords—E-flat major with its lowered VII and altered IV—are used, then a scale fragment in Liszt-like division of the two hands based on D, concluding in D major. The vocal part sustains the D throughout all six measures (Example 54).

No preparation is made for the IV-I plagal cadence which ends "La Carpe" from *Le Bestiaire*. The IV degree appears in measure 10, as it has on four previous occasions, in root position minus the third, preceded by V, also incomplete. This time it progresses to

plus qu'aux coeurs,

sans ralentir

Example 54. "La belle jeunesse" from *Chansons Gaillardes*, measures 69–76. Copyright 1926 by Heugel, Paris. Used by permission.

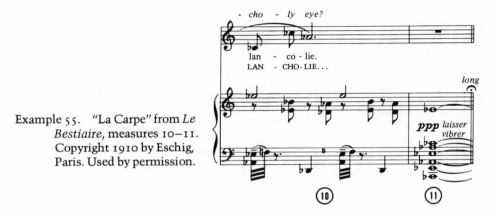

Example 55. "La Carpe" from *Le Bestiaire*, measures 10–11. Copyright 1910 by Eschig, Paris. Used by permission.

a full A-flat minor triad, the only complete harmony found in the piano accompaniment (Example 55).

The tritone bass progression B-F of "Chanson d'Orkenise" from *Banalités* is a deviation from the standard IV-I cadence. The B clashing with the C of the voice line, which implies dominant, is sustained over gliding 7 and $^6_4$ chords in the right hand and resolves to the I. All comes to rest on the open fifth, F-C (Example 56).

Appropriate to "L'Écrevisse" from *Le Bestiaire* is the final cadence II-I. The

Example 56.   "Chanson d'Or-
            kenise" from *Banalités*,
            measures 51–57. Copyright
            1941 by Eschig, Paris. Used
            by permission.

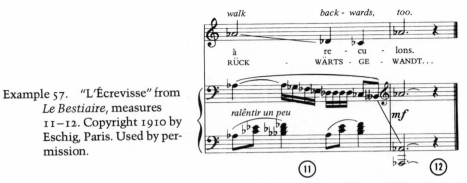

Example 57. "L'Écrevisse" from *Le Bestiaire*, measures 11–12. Copyright 1910 by Eschig, Paris. Used by permission.

neapolitan alteration is employed, and the cadence is repeated six times above a descending scale (Example 57).

A neapolitan effect is found in "1904" from *Quatre Poèmes*. The closing is estab-

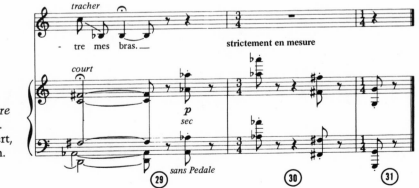

Example 58. "1904" from *Quatre Poèmes*, measures 29–31. Copyright 1931 by Salabert, Paris. Used by permission.

lished by an authentic cadence (with lowered fifth of the V⁷). This A flat creates the neapolitan, especially when it is isolated before the end (Example 58).

Some examples of unusual cadential devices may be seen in "Les gars qui vont à la fête" from *Chansons Villageoises*, which relies upon F major to an unusual degree

Example 59. "Les gars qui vont à la fête" from *Chansons Villageoises*, measures 42–45. Copyright 1943 by Eschig, Paris. Used by permission.

throughout. Before the end, however, interruptions by neapolitan sixths with their dominant and chromatically gliding chords appear (measure 42). The traditional cadence V-I closes the piece, again preceded by the neapolitan (lowered second), as in the previous example. Texture is thinned to a single note in the final measure, where the V (C) is heard again in the piano. The neapolitan C flat appears once more, but it is quickly returned by the repeated V (C) in both voice and piano, finally coming to a standstill on the I with an open fifth (Example 59).

As in all of Poulenc's writing, added color tones play an important role in the cadences. The vocal line establishes G major in the concluding four measures of "Le Lac" ("Jezioro") from *Huit Chansons Polonaises*. In the accompaniment, the right hand adds A sharp, the left hand F sharp to the final chord. The preceding C minor indicates a plagal cadence; the next chord—A sharp⁷ (with C)—is a preparation for the final (Example 60).

Example 60. "Le Lac" ("Jezioro") from *Huit Chansons Polonaises*, measures 28–31. Copyright 1934 by Salabert, Paris. Used by permission.

Example 61. "Nous avons fait la nuit" from *Tel Jour Telle Nuit*, measures 46–47. Copyright 1937 by Durand, Paris. Used by permission.

In keeping with his fondness for the cabaret style, Poulenc often colors his harmony with "blue" notes on flatted third, fifth, or seventh scale degrees. The last song of the cycle *Tel Jour Telle Nuit*, "Nous avons fait la nuit," cadences with the traditional

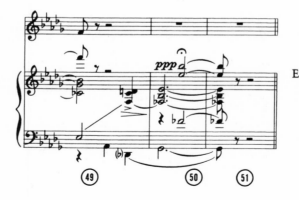

Example 62. "C'est le joli printemps" from *Chansons Villageoises*, measures 49–51. Copyright 1943 by Eschig, Paris. Used by permission.

IV-V-I formula in C, but with flatted third and seventh "blues" added to the final (Example 61).

"C'est le joli printemps" from *Chansons Villageoises* cadences on G flat, the subdominant of D flat, with an added sixth (E flat) and F flat forming impure octaves as in the preceding chord—D flat verses D (Example 62).

Modulations

The traditional means of modulation are by common chords (pivot chords), enharmonic change, and by voice leading, mostly chromatic. These occur in the songs sporadically, but free juxtaposition of keys is seen more frequently.

In extended modulations the harmonies not only remain in the new key for some time, but the signatures are also changed. Such is the case in only a few instances, notably "Sanglots" from *Banalités*, which opens with sixteen measures in F-sharp minor and modulates by means of enharmonic change into E-flat minor at measure 17. The F sharp and C sharp of F-sharp minor become the G flat and D flat respectively of the new key, E-flat minor. The key signature changes to that of the new tonality which is in effect for forty-seven measures before returning to the original F-sharp minor (Example 63).

Example 63. "Sanglots" from
Banalités, measures 15–17.
Copyright 1941 by Eschig,
Paris. Used by permission.

Example 64. "La belle jeunesse"
from *Chansons Gaillardes*,
measures 25–28. Copyright
1926 by Heugel, Paris. Used
by permission.

"La belle jeunesse" from *Chansons Gaillardes* affords another example of Poulenc's rarely employed extended modulations. In measure 26, B-flat major is gradually reached after the existing D major of the opening section. B-flat major becomes the predominant tonality in measure 27, and with the change of key signature from D major to B-flat major in measure 28, the modulation is effected (Example 64).

Example 65, "Bonne Journée" from *Tel Jour Telle Nuit*, achieves modulation by different means. The E-flat minor leads, by means of stepwise bass progression, to a D-F sharp-A flat-C-E flat chord, using the common tone G flat as F sharp. This chord, a minor dominant ninth with altered fifth, is followed by a fleeting dominant on G, which leads to C major. In this section enharmonic change is combined with modulation in the circle of fifths, D-G-C.

The juxtaposition of extratonal chords, which is so common in Poulenc's harmony, does not always give the feeling of a new tonality and cannot qualify as genuine modulation. However, some of these juxtapositions or detours follow conventional patterns.

The temporary juxtaposition of keys in the mediant relationship provides another method of detouring from the tonality. In the case of "Air Vif" from *Airs Chantés* (*Moréas*) it is accomplished by means of enharmonic changes. A detour from E-flat minor to C-sharp minor is made by spelling the E-flat minor III triad (C flat–B double flat–D flat) enharmoncially (F sharp–A–C sharp) to become the subdominant of C-

Example 65. "Bonne Journée" from *Tel Jour Telle Nuit*, measures 21–29. Copyright 1937 by Durand, Paris. Used by permission.

Poulenc's Songs 108

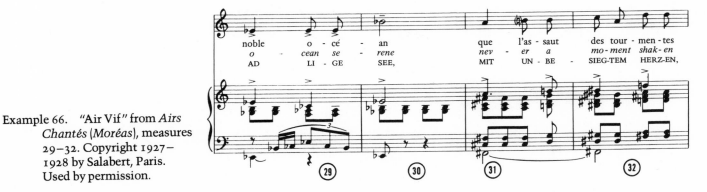

Example 66. "Air Vif" from *Airs Chantés (Moréas)*, measures 29–32. Copyright 1927–1928 by Salabert, Paris. Used by permission.

sharp minor, which remains in effect only eight measures before encountering another detour (Example 66).

Chromatic progressions offer still another choice for momentary excursion into other keys, as in "Au delà" from *Trois Poèmes de Louise Vilmorin*, where for a brief four measures (33–36) B-flat minor follows immediately a more extensive section in B major. The intervening D minor provides the connection (Example 67).

Gliding or side-stepping is another means of juxtaposition by chromatic step. The B-flat minor tonality in "Paul Klee" from *Le Travail du Peintre* is established in measures 24–25 with a V-I progression. This is followed abruptly by V-I in A minor, mea-

Example 67. "Au delà" from *Trois Poèmes de Louise Vilmorin*, measures 30–35. Copyright 1931 by Durand, Paris. Used by permission.

sures 26-27, producing the effect of sliding almost imperceptibly from one key to an adjacent one (Example 68).

Poulenc often merely obscures the key center rather than modulating or even de-

Example 68. "Paul Klee" from *Le Travail du Peintre*, measures 24–27. Copyright 1956 by Eschig, Paris. Used by permission.

touring momentarily. This he may do with floating tonality that fails to establish any specific key center. In "L'Espionne" from *Calligrammes*, the bass sequence in measures 17–20 (B flat to E flat; G sharp to C sharp; F sharp to B; E to A) through transposition is harmonized differently each time, thus never being committed to a definite key (Example 69).

Example 69. "L'Espionne" from *Calligrammes*, measures 17–20. Copyright 1948 by Heugel, Paris. Used by permission.

111   Harmony

Due to the incorporation of extratonal chords in most of the diatonic fabric, the feeling for definite modulatory changes is not often present. It is rather a continous mixture of tertian chords in various keys.

Nonharmonic Tones and Dissonances

In diatonic harmony, dissonances often are created by nonharmonic tones. Poulenc, too, employs them mostly in his diatonic passages according to the strict rules.

Passing tones, both accented and unaccented, are numerous and are also frequently chromatically altered. They appear in both the vocal line and accompaniment.

In measures 44–45 of "Air Champêtre" from *Airs Chantés* we find the typical appoggiatura (C to B) as melody in the piano four times (Example 70).

Example 70. "Air Champêtre" from *Airs Chantés (Moréas)*, measures 44–46. Copyright 1927–1928 by Salabert, Paris. Used by permission.

Example 71. "A son page" from *Poèmes de Ronsard*, measures 45–47. Copyright 1925 by Heugel, Paris. Used by permission.

A series of appoggiaturas with échappées in a sequence of descending seventh chords adds to the character of the presto in the coda in "A son page" from *Poèmes de Ronsard*, measures 45–46 (Example 71).

Prepared and resolved suspensions are sparingly used. However, free dissonances carried over the barline give the aural impact of suspensions. Some suspended dissonances are resolved in different voices and appear entirely free.

Throughout "Violon" from *Fiançailles Pour Rire*, the accompaniment assumes the character of the violin. The appoggiaturas and suspensions outline the melodic figure of the cambiata in measures 33–36 (Example 72).

Anticipations occur under the same circumstances as suspensions, but appear only rarely.

The category of nonharmonic tones may be extended to include all the seconds, fourths, sixths, etc., used chiefly for enrichment of color, and also to the mixture of the chords within the same key. These are the main characteristics of Poulenc's harmony.

S'offre a l'a - mour___ comme un fruit___

Example 72. "Violon" from *Fiançailles Pour Rire*, measures 33–36. Copyright 1940 by Salabert, Paris. Used by permission.

Conclusion

Poulenc in his harmony emerges confidently dependent upon traditional diatonic foundations and structures. However, each song becomes unique as the composer selects the precise harmonic style or device to bring musical sonority into the closest possible proximity to the word and the aesthetic intent of the poetry. He is constantly shifting tonalities, adding color tones to transform traditional chords into more complex sounds, simultaneously working with consonance and dissonance, yet keeping strict control with strong diatonic underpinnings and the consistent and reliable return to diatonic cadences. What results from this inventive use of harmonic devices from all eras are compositions of solid traditional technique embellished by unexpected sonorities. Rich imagination and the eclectic harmonic vocabulary create the discernible "Poulenc style."

V Form

        Consideration of poetry determines the architecture of Poulenc's songs, the form being controlled by the demands of the text as are harmony and melody. Length, as well as specific structure, is dependent on the poetry. As to form types, Poulenc remains conservative, since he uses the traditional binary and ternary structures as well as through-composed and free sectional organization. He manipulates all with ease, often with originality.

        Poulenc rarely alters the poems he selects. Omission of verses or reiteration of lines are avoided. He builds the music exactly to their dimensions. Thus his shortest song, "La Sauterelle" from *Le Bestiaire*, comprises only four measures. Other songs of this set are also in small dimension: eight, eleven, twelve, and thirteen measures, respectively. Only one is forty-three bars long. Variety of length within a set is not unusual, but rather the rule.

        The most extended of the Poulenc songs is the setting of Apollinaire's "L'Anguille." It fills one hundred measures without introduction or interludes, but there is a nineteen-measure postlude. Other major songs are "Couplets Bachiques" from *Chansons Gaillardes* (ninety-one measures) and "Paganini" from *Métamorphoses* (eighty-nine measures). The majority of songs extend between forty and sixty bars. As the dimension of each song is predetermined by the length of unaltered poems, the challenge rests in the exigencies of structures. They can be broadly divided into open and closed types. Before discussing these, some aggregates which do not fit the conventional mold should be noted.

Transitional Forms

Parallel periods or phrase groups are usually selected for the extremely short songs. However, "Le Chèvre du Thibet" from *Le Bestiaire*, a song of only nine bars, is irregularly organized: two unequal phrases of two bars are followed by a one-bar interlude. Three bars (1 + 2) end the song. In these two unequal sections is neither thematic repetition nor rhythmic parallellism. The impression of free narration is created and enhanced by the narrow range and intervals of the voice line.

In the same group, "Le Dauphin" has an introduction of four bars (2 × 2), followed by the melody which is periodical:

a	*b*		*a*	*c*	
2 + 2			2 + 2 +1		

The last segment is larger (three bars), and the two bars of the interlude are repeated as postlude. The rudimentary organization is binary.

"L'Écrevisse," another song from *Le Bestiaire*, is irregular. After a two-bar introduction follows a phrase group of 2 + 1½ bars. The second section begins with a varied repeat of the first two bars of the melody. The last segment in augmented note values is repeated but separated by a rest.

Prelude	a	plus	a¹
2 (x)	2 + 1½		2 + 2 + 2
			(augmented)
			(x) in piano

"La Carpe," the last song in the group, is more regular. The introduction (two bars) and all four phrases are of the same length (two measures).

"Un Poème," of Apollinaire, contains a four-measure (2 + 2) introduction followed by the same four-bar segment in the voice. A three-bar phrase is followed by 2 × 2 bars.

Introduction	Voice	Postlude
2 + 2	a (4) (2 + 2) plus b (3) plus a¹ (4) (2 + 2)	2

The melodic relations are more obvious in the piano than in the voice part.

"Invocation aux Parques" from *Chansons Gaillardes* has an eight-bar introduction:

117   Form

Prelude (8)	a (4)	b (4)	c (4)	Postlude (3)
(2 + 2 + 2 + 2)	(2 + 2)	(2 + 2)	(2 + 2)	(2 + 1)

The melody consists of three phrase groups of four measures each, and a two-bar postlude with close.

Regular Binary Forms

Two sections of equal length and containing the same material are used mainly in Poulenc's folk songs. "L'Adieu" from *Huit Chansons Polonaises* is such an example. The form is 4 + 4 bars (first stanza). This unit is exactly repeated, first in the voice, then as postlude in the piano, but set an octave higher.

"Les Gars Polonais," also from *Huit Chansons Polonaises*, is strophic, too. There is no introduction. The melody consists of two regular periods, each eight measures long. The second is in slower tempo. The whole sixteen bars are repeated literally.

"Le Lac," of the same set, is another example of binary form, but with two unequal sections. *A* has six bars (3 + 3); *B* has three subsections (3 + 4 + 3). The introduction is four bars long. However, the third bar is shortened.

These folk songs yield another type of binary structure with "Le Drapeau Blanc." Here, the *A* section is eight measures (4 + 4); the last four bars of the *B* section are repeated (petit reprise)—8 + 4. The postlude is four bars long. The scheme is:

A (8)	B (12)	plus	*Postlude* (4)
(4 + 4)	(4 + 4 + 4)		
	repeated		

An example of rounded binary occurs in the second song from *Huit Chansons Polonaises,* "Le Départ." It is designed:

A (12)		B (16)	
a	b	c	b
4 + 8 (4 +4)		(4 + 4) plus 8 (4 + 4)	

"La Maîtresse Volage" from *Chansons Gaillardes* is in compound binary form, the large sections being subdivided into smaller subsections. The scheme is:

Prelude (8)

A	
a (7)	b (9)
2 + 2 + 2 + 1 (¾)	2 + (1 + 1) + 2 + 3

B	
a¹ (7)	b¹ (13)
2 + 2 + 2 + 1 (¾)	2 + 2 + (the last 9 bars
(melodically	identical with b)
different)	

The *B* section is longer by four measures which are accounted for in the second section (measures 34–37).

Ternary Forms

The ternary structures may be classified according to several organizations. One thematic unit may return three times in more or less varied shape. Either pitch changes or transpositions distinguish this type from strophic organization. Most common is the return of the first section after a contrasting middle part. However three different sections may be joined together. The strict bar form (two Stollen plus Abgesang) does not appear, though two similar sections may follow each other. Composite ternary structures with subdivisions (usually two) are not infrequent. The length of the three units is generally equal, but shorter middle parts or truncated repeats of the first section occur.

   The group *Fiançailles Pour Rire* yields one example of the same material in all sections, "Le Dame d'André." Preceded by three bars of introduction, the initial two-bar phrase of the vocal part is transposed at the beginning of the second section and transposed again at the beginning of the third section. However, much of the rest in sections two and three is new. The song ends with four measures of postlude. The scheme is:

Prelude (3)	plus	A (8)	plus	Interlude (2)	plus
		4 + 2 + 2			

A¹ (14)	plus	A² (12)	plus	Postlude (4)
4 + 2 + 1 + 1 + 2 + 1 + 1 + 2		4 + 2 + 2 + 2 + 2		

The regular A B A types are often subdivided, and "Couplets Bachiques" from *Chansons Gaillardes* clearly shows this technique. The large parts differ in key. The A-flat major is abandoned in the modulatory middle section. Five bars of prelude introduce the first section, A (thirty bars). This segment is divided into two subparts (18 + 12) which start with the same four bars as the third part of the song. The whole thirty bars are literally repeated, and a coda of five bars is added. Section B is shorter (twenty measures) and consists of two bar groups. Only the end (back modulation) is extended. The same beginning of both A subsections justifies the title "Couplets." The scheme is:

Prelude (5)

A (30)

a (18)	a¹ (12)
4 + 8 + 2 + 4	4 + 2 + 1 + 1 + 2 + 2

first 4 bars the same

	B (20)	
6 + 2 + 4	plus (4)	then re-transition (4)

	A (30)	
	exactly the same as beginning	

Coda (5)

"La Belle Jeunesse," also from this set, is another extended ternary song. Here the middle part is also subdivided, contrasting in vocal style (cantabile versus parlando) and equal in length with the material of *A*. The repeated main part is partly transposed from D to A, but later returns to the original key. Some units are left out; some appear twice. The last note of the melody is extended for six measures. The scheme is:

	A (21)	
a (12)		*b* (9)
1 + 1 + 1 + 1 +	2 bars interlude	2 + 2 + 1 + 1 + 3
2 + 2 + 2 + 2		

B (21)

c (13)
6 + 2 + 2 + 3

c^1 (8)
2 + 2 + 2 + 2

Interlude of 3 bars (transposed prelude)

A (19)

exact repetition, partly transposed

a (9)
1 + 1 + 1 + 1 +
2 + 3

2 bars interlude

b (10)
2 + 2 + 1 + 2 + 3
almost exact

Coda (5)

extension of 5 bars (sustained note)

Other examples of the A B A type are "Dernier Poème de Robert Desnos" and "Adelina à la Promenade," from the set of *Trois Chansons de Garcia-Lorca*.

The ternary form in "Chanson à Boire," the second song of *Chansons Gaillardes*, is rudimentary, as only parts of the beginning section return two bars from its middle, then the first three with an added different ending. The scheme is outlined thusly:

Prelude (7)	A (9)	B (8)	A¹ (10)	Close (1)
	3 + 2 + 2 + 2	2 + 2 + 4	2 + 2 + 3 + 2 + 1	

Poulenc sometimes selects three distinctly different units for the ternary form, preferring poems of more fluidity which adapt themselves to this treatment.

Connected by similarity of contour, "Voyage à Paris" from *Banalités* is an example. The three units are of equal length with the ten measures of prelude balanced by the eight-bar postlude. In the three distinct sections, only similarities of contour are noticeable. Again the tonal regions of the middle section are different. The scheme:

Prelude	A	B	Interlude	C	Postlude
10	16	16	7	16	8

"Dans l'Herbe" from *Fiançailles Pour Rire* is an example of compact three-unit ternary form. It is divided into sections of 12–6–12 measures, each containing distinctly new material; only the declamatory style is the same. There is no prelude nor any transition dividing the sections. A postlude extends the song for only three cadential measures. Such blunt compactness is not characteristic of Poulenc, but rather is exceptional.

Other examples of similar structure occur in the songs "Chanson Bretonne" from *Cinq Poèmes de Max Jacob*, "L'Espionne" from *Calligrammes*, and "Marc Chagall" from *Le Travail du Peintre*.

Atypical Closed Forms

More than three formal units in songs are not frequent. One case is found in "Il Vole" from *Fiançailles Pour Rire*:

A	A¹	Transition	B	Transition	C	Transition	A¹
6	7	4 (2 + 2)	8	4	8	5	9

This structure accommodates five sections built upon similar rhythmic and melodic material and three transitional sections that contain the text refrain.

Somewhat related to the multi-unit organization is the rondo. Poulenc uses it in a very condensed way in the first of the Polish songs, "La Couronne." This is closer to the French rondeau than the classic type, since the refrain does not return immediately after the first couplet section. It is planned in the so-called five-part (two themes) form. It is diagrammed:

Prelude	A	B		Ending
9	8	4+4	(piano)	4
	2 + 2	2 + 2	2 + 2	1 + 1 + 1 + 1
	2 + 2			

A^1	B^1	A	Postlude
8	4 + 4 (piano)	8	11
(transposed)		(original)	4 + 4 + 3

Open Forms

Poulenc prefers sectional composition to pure through-composed style. Even in the short songs, where one would not look for subdivision, he is most apt to repeat motives or reiterate motivic fragments. There are some purely through-composed songs, however. "Plume d'eau Claire" from *Cinq Poèmes de Paul Eluard* is a nine-measure song of this type, lyric in concept.

Another is "C'est ainsi que tu es" from *Métamorphoses*. Here, the prelude material provides fragments for the melody to follow, but each strophe of the poem shows different musical treatment. The song's continuity is preserved despite meter changes that occur during the eighteen-measure span of the song.

One of Poulenc's most performed songs, "Je n'ai envie que de t'aimer" of *Tel Jour Telle Nuit*, is through-composed. Its driving rhythm, meter changes, and major-minor mode alterations heighten its élan rather than drive wedges between strophes; cohesion is maintained throughout eighteen measures of constantly new material.

"La Souris" from *Deux Mélodies, 1956*, an Apollinaire poem, is an eleven-measure song based on a triadic melodic aggregate alternating with free declamation. Prelude and postlude are reminiscent of each other.

Other songs in open forms are sectional. The composer seems to prefer new material for each verse of a poem, but without continuity or solidity. In these sectional compositions, he employs contrast without maintaining the same tempo, rhythm, or melody.

Typical of this organization is "Berceuse" from *Cinq Poèmes de Max Jacob*, based on a cabaret melody, but strictly sectionalized. The diagram is:

A	Interlude	B	C	D	Postlude
16	2	16	16	17	7
				(4+4+2+1+3+3)	

The sections are different in character: *A* (lyric); *B* (chromatic in stepwise motion); *C* (quasi-declamatory); and *D* (again chromatic with small intervals).

"Sanglots" from *Banalités* is also sectional, containing five units in different keys. A double bar separates *A* from *B* and *C* from *D* to emphasize the sectional quality. The plan of this song is:

Prelude	A	B	C	D	E	Postlude
7	9	10	13	20	17	2
	F-sharp minor	E-flat minor	B-flat minor	E-flat minor	F-sharp minor	

Other sectional songs similarly constructed are "Hôtel" from *Banalités*, "Vers le Sud" from *Calligrammes*, and "Paul Klee" and "Joan Miro" from *Le Travail du Peintre*.

In general, Poulenc continues to use well-established compositional organization. He adapts purely musical structures to the poetry of his choice and adjusts them. He does not invent new formal devices. Sometimes the simplicity of the structure is obvious, often deceptive. This is independent from the length of the song. Often certain formal expectations are met, but Poulenc can never be taken for granted. Paramount is his fidelity to the poet. He never distorts words or intent. This governs the selection of forms for the songs. Structure serves the text, and if anything must yield, it is the music, not the poetry.

VI Piano Accompaniment

Pianist and singer share equally in the musical demands of Poulenc's songs. Even where the accompaniment is technically simple, it enhances the content of text and melody. Many songs, however, are extremely taxing for the pianist. Digital virtuosity and subtleties of weight and stress distribution are required for many passages, chord sequences in rhythmic shifts, often occurring at blazing speed. Lyric sensitivity is also imperative, for Poulenc frequently presents the melody in the piano which must sing beneath the declamatory vocal line. Many times color is engendered by pedal instructions which are precise. Little leeway is given in regard to tempo selection, as metronome markings are always indicated and reinforced by verbal instructions.

The patterns of accompaniment which the composer selects are sometimes steady and sustained throughout with little deviation. More often, however, types of designs are mixed, varying in sonority, density, and rhythm. Notable, too, is the use of extreme keyboard ranges. These devices are frequently arbitrary, applied for musical reasons alone. Then the whole accompaniment assumes kaleidoscopic diversity, and the changes occur often, even after only a few bars.

Cases where the vocal line is doubled by the piano are frequent, but they often last only a short time. Transparency is also achieved when there are two lines—one following the voice, the other accompanying—although this occurs only sporadically. When the piano setting is in two parts, Poulenc almost never uses equal independent lines, but rather a mixture between one melody (either in upper or lower voice) and figuration. To this two-part setting of the piano, a third line is furnished by the voice.

Much more common is writing in free style where lines are mixed with chords or figures. The chords are used in various rhythms, either straight or dissolved into various components achieving a full sound. The figurations range from simple arpeggios and scales to more complicated invented patterns. In general, the mixture between chordal aggregates and more rapid passages creates a feeling of virtuosity, reinforced by numerous octave doublings of bass and melody. This occurs not only in independent piano sections such as preludes and postludes, but often throughout the songs, making it most important for the singer to preserve the clarity of the vocal line. In this, the composer often aids the singer by duplicating the voice in the piano. This can be done in unison, but often an octave higher or lower, respectively. These doublings are sometimes continued throughout the greater part of the whole composition; sometimes they cease after a few bars, especially when the piano melody becomes independent. Quite frequently support of the vocal line occurs at rhythmically accentuated pivot points or on chords.

Several songs use the stereotyped accompaniment of different dances, while some display special sound effects. These can be created by imitation of other instruments or

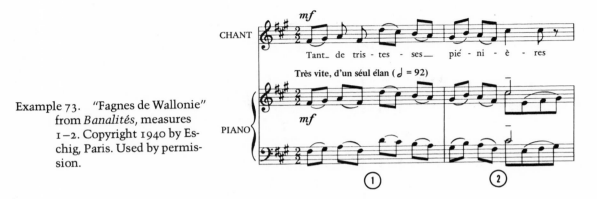

Example 73. "Fagnes de Wallonie" from *Banalités*, measures 1–2. Copyright 1940 by Eschig, Paris. Used by permission.

extramusical elements. The pedal, which, as in all French music, is used in discriminating and sensitive ways, is an important factor of the piano sonority.

The following excerpts exemplify different styles of accompaniment. Unison between melody and accompaniment is found in "Fagnes de Wallonie" from *Banalités* for the first two bars (Example 73).

In the following four bars, some independent notes for the piano are inserted without destroying the lean sound. After this the texture becomes more dense, as is typical in many Poulenc songs.

In "Le Pont," one line in the accompaniment is added to the melody for the first seven bars. From bar 8 on, the accompaniment is split between the bass notes on the strong beats and accompanying figures in the right hand. Three-part writing occurs

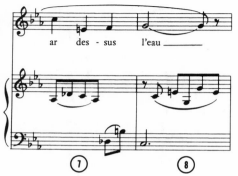

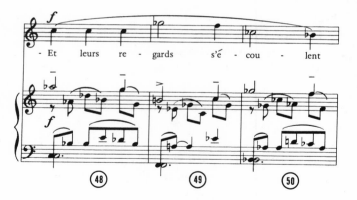

Example 74. "Le Pont," measures
1–2, 7–8 and 48–50.
Copyright 1946 by Eschig,
Paris. Used by permission.

Poulenc's Songs 132

Example 75. "Madrigal" from *Chansons Gaillardes*, measures 18–19. Copyright 1926 by Heugel, Paris. Used by permission.

often in the course of this song. Later (bars 48—50) the sound is made fuller by adding another melody line in the piano, a different middle voice (Example 74).

The fast tempo of "Paganini" from *Métamorphoses* does not allow many doublings. Throughout the three lines, the figures in the right hand and the bass are sustained. This song will be discussed later as characteristic of sound imitation.

Single chords accompanying the melody appear often in "Madrigal" from *Chansons Gaillardes* (Example 75). To avoid monotony, however, scale figures in the right hand are added later.

The use of chords is more diversified in "Couplets Bachiques" from the same group, where they not only underscore the doubling of the melody but contribute to the density of the sound (Example 76). In this song the accompaniment is more elaborate, as numerous scale passages and figures appear in both the right and left hands. The sixteenth-note motion is often sustained, breaking the chords in the middle voices.

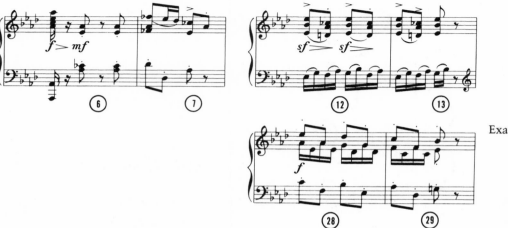

Example 76. "Couplets Bachiques" from *Chansons
Gaillardes*, measures 6–7,
12–13, and 28–29. Copy-
right 1926 by Heugel, Paris.
Used by permission.

Two-chord sequences form the motive in "La Souris" from *Deux Mélodies 1956*.
They are connected by arpeggiating eighth notes (Example 77).

Arpeggiated chords combined with melody and bass are frequently found—for instance, in "Main dominée par le coeur" (Example 78).

Doubling

The cases where the voice line is doubled in the piano, at least for parts of whole songs,
are numerous. Poulenc displays ingenuity in subtle varieties of this principle.

Example 77.   "La Souris" from
          Deux Mélodies 1956, mea-
          sures 1–2. Copyright 1956
          by Eschig, Paris. Used by
          permission.

pp

beaucoup de pédale

Example 78.   "Main dominée par
          le coeur," measures 23–24.
          Copyright 1947 by Salabert,
          Paris. Used by permission.

marqué

Ici, on ne mettra jamais assez de pédale

In "Voyage" from *Calligrammes*, the melody is doubled in unison plus the lower octave, and the middle voice is restricted to syncopated notes, also in octaves. In the middle part of the song, however, the type of accompaniment changes, as the reinforced melody is supported by repeated chords in eighth notes in the middle above a harmonic bass (Example 79).

In "Le Dauphin" from *Le Bestiaire*, the melody is doubled in unison, played by the left hand throughout. The accompaniment lies in the right hand and is placed in the high register above the melody.

135   **Piano Accompaniment**

Example 79. "Voyage" from *Calligrammes*, measures 1–3 and 21–22. Copyright 1948 by Heugel, Paris. Used by permission.

Example 80. "Attributs" from *Poèmes de Ronsard*, measures 9 and 12–13. Copyright 1924–1925 by Heugel, Paris. Used by permission.

Doubling of the melody is found also in "Attributs" from *Poèmes de Ronsard*. Here it appears in the beginning in octaves plus thirds and chords, later with just a simple accompanying figure of broken chords (Example 80).

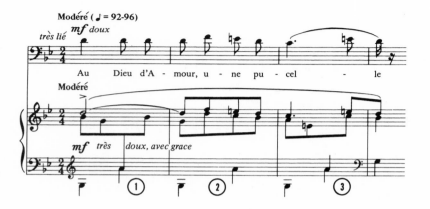

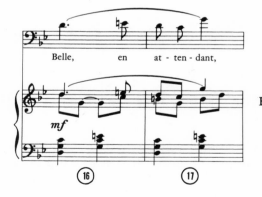

Example 81. "L'Offrande" from *Chansons Gaillardes*, measures 1–3 and 16–17. Copyright 1926 by Heugel, Paris. Used by permission.

In "L'Offrande" from *Chansons Gaillardes*, written for the bass voice, the doubling occurs an octave higher, sometimes with added thirds. The bass plays the harmonic fundamentals in steady quarter notes. Throughout this short song, this device is sustained; later, however, the bass moves in full chords continuing through the postlude (Example 81). This song is characteristic for its steady rhythmic pulse of eighth notes.

An interesting case is "Nuage" from *Deux Mélodies 1956*. Here, in the beginning, the doubling occurs an octave lower in the middle voice. The regular quarter notes in the bass and the syncopated thirds provide the harmony. In this piece the principle of doubling changes later; the texture not only becomes thicker, but the melodic tones occur in pivot chords on the accentuated beats and the harmonies become more complex. Poulenc's tendency to increase the fullness of sound as the song proceeds is obvious here, as may be seen in the last two parts of the example (Example 82).

Doubling the melody plus a variegated accompaniment sometimes results in a delicate sound picture. In "Reine des Mouettes" from *Métamorphoses*, repeated bass chords in upbeat rhythm and sixteenth-note arpeggios in the middle provide a steady motoric motion which is sustained, though the doubling of the voice is not strictly observed throughout (Example 83).

A similar sound pattern, only in slow tempo, is found in "C'est ainsi que tu es," also from *Métamorphoses*. Here the motion is in eighth notes; sometimes two middle voices, sometimes even chords are added to the doubled melody and the bass. The

Example 82. "Nuage" from *Deux Mélodies 1956*, measures 5–6, 9, 15, and 20. Copyright 1956 by Eschig, Paris. Used by permission.

Example 83. "Reine des Mouettes" from *Métamorphoses*, measure 1. Copyright 1943 by Salabert, Paris. Used by permission.

interval of the doubling changes here between the unison and the higher octave (Example 84).

Somewhat intermittent is the doubling in "A Son Page" from *Poèmes de Ron-*

Example 84. "C'est ainsi que tu es" from *Métamorphoses*, measures 5–6. Copyright 1943 by Salabert, Paris. Used by permission.

141   **Piano Accompaniment**

sard. In the beginning, the doubled melody is accompanied only by short, lean chords, later by full harmonies, sometimes only fragmentary. Here the different texture is motivated by the handling of the text, though the bulk of this long song is homogeneous.

Dances

Due to the composer's penchant for folk and popular music, quite a few of his songs show accompaniments in the rhythm and character of dances. The waltz is prominent, either in explicit form or by application of its stereotype beat. According to tradition, the tempo of these waltzes changes considerably. Naturally, the mazurka is prominent in the Polish songs. A sarabande and a lively march are also found.

In its most traditional form the waltz accompaniment is used in "Voyage à Paris" from *Banalités*, even indicated in the composer's marking (see page 66). Here, the voice line forms the melody. The tempo is fast, so the whole bar is the unit, marked by the composer "à 1 temps."

In "Amoureuses" from *Cinq Poèmes de Paul Eluard*, a steady waltzlike rhythm (marked by the composer) indicates the rocking of the cradle.

The entire group of *Huit Chansons Polonaises*, folksong arrangements, contains dance rhythms. Obviously, the national mazurka is most frequently represented (six times), once, in "Le Départ," specifically marked as such. Five of these mazurkas are in the traditional slow tempo, even if marked ⅜ instead of ¾ meter, as in "Le Drapeau Blanc." The first song, "Le Couronne," is very fast ("Preste et enjoué") and could almost be considered a waltz would it not be for the typical mazurka ♪. ♪♩ ♩ | ♩ ♩ rhythm. Two of the songs, "Les Gars Polonais" and "La Vistule," are polkas, both animated and gay. In the majority of these songs, the right hand of the piano doubles the melody sporadically with added figurations. Sometimes the piano plays only the dance accompaniment.

The heading "Movement de marche enlevée" and the constant march rhythm fit the text of "Le retour du sergent" from *Chansons Villageoises*. Staccato and legato chords alternate without ever abandoning the military stance (Example 85). The imitation of marching in this song, like the imitation in the previously mentioned "Berceuse," represent songs in which the sound is conditioned by the text. This is still more obvious in the following two pieces associated with violin and guitar.

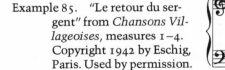

Example 85. "Le retour du sergent" from *Chansons Villageoises*, measures 1–4. Copyright 1942 by Eschig, Paris. Used by permission.

143   **Piano Accompaniment**

Special Sonorities

The song "Paganini" from *Métamorphoses* imitates violin virtuosity through high speed and violinistic figures in the right hand in broken arpeggios, sometimes runs (Example 86). The composer, aware of the difficulty, even marks some of them with fingering. Chords, reminding one of violin double stops, are inserted three times for good measure.

As noted previously, the right hand of the piano in "Violon" from *Fiançailles Pour Rire* is a sound imitation of constant violin double stops. Broken chordal rhythms imitate the change of strings. A cadenzalike run and a new motive at the end of the song are also violinistic in character. The last staccato note is marked "quasi pizz."

Example 86. "Paganini" from *Métamorphoses*, measures 1–5. Copyright 1943 by Salabert, Paris. Used by permission.

"A Sa Guitare" is written for harp or piano accompaniment. Here, exact sound imitations are restricted to the prelude and postlude, where strumming and rapid runs are characterized. In the middle part, broken chords signify either harp or guitar sound.

An incidental extramusical sound imitation is the three-times returning bird chirping in the song "Nuage" from *Deux Mélodies 1956*, conditioned by the text, in contrast to the steady motion of the whole piece (Example 87).

The piano sound in general is shaded by various applications of the pedals. Pierre Bernac stated, "Poulenc always asked for ample use of the pedal in the piano part."[1] The composer himself rememberd he learned this from his friend and teacher Ricardo Viñes: "No one could teach the art of using the pedals, an essential feature of modern piano music, better than Viñes. He somehow managed to extract clarity precisely from the ambiguities of the pedals."[2] Hardly any composer is more explicit in pedalling instructions. Even the lack of it is indicated "sans pédale." When the pedal is used, sometimes elaborate remarks guide the performer. "Tu Vois le Feu du Soir" of *Miroirs Brûlants* provides a sample of these instructions: "Toute la mélodie sera accompagnée dans un halo

Example 87. "Nuage" from *Deux Mélodies 1956*, measure 17. Copyright 1956 by Eschig, Paris. Used by permission.

de pédales; le chant doucement en dehors" ("The entire song should be accompanied in a halo of pedals; the vocal line softly coming through").

In "Enfant de Troupe" from *Cocardes*, Poulenc advises the pianist to play "les deux pédales" (damper plus mute). "Vers le Sud" from *Calligrammes* carries the instructions "Toute cette mélodie sera baignée de pédale; les batteries étant à peine effleurées" ("The entire song to be bathed in pedal; the rhythmic accents hardly touched"). "Il Pleut" from the same group is marked "Aussi vite que possible, très rythmé dans une buée de pédale" ("As fast as possible, very rhythmic in a mist of pedal"). "Sanglots" of *Banalitiés*: "Durant toute cette mélodie, se servir beaucoup des Pédales" ("Throughout this song use a lot of pedal"); "Jouer de bugle" from *Parisiana*: "Doucement ponctué mais avec beaucoup de pédale" ("Softly accentuated but with much pedal"). Plainly, Debussy's influence is felt in Poulenc's pedalling.

Independent Use of the Piano

Compared with the number of songs that lack solo sections for the piano, those with preludes and postludes are in the minority. No generalization can be made about the length and the content of them, nor is there any regular relationship between postludes or preludes, as many songs have only one of them. Neither can one generalize about the content which may or may not be related to the melodies of the songs.

The preludes vary from those which measure a few bars containing only the harmonic and rhythmic background or the initial theme of the song to more elaborate types. These may be based on the principal melody which is anticipated in its entire length or may even contain material which later does not appear.

In "Marc Chagall" from *Le Travail du Peintre*, the whole principal theme plus an extended cadence appears in twelve bars (see pages 68–9).

In "Madrigal" from *Chansons Gaillardes*, the main eight-bar melody is quoted, followed by an independent extension of four bars which never returns, plus a concluding segment of four bars, also not reappearing. No postlude at all balances this introduction.

The prelude to "A Sa Guitare" contains the sound effects mentioned on page 145. It is not used again during the song except in the last two bars, where it appears modified and shortened to one bar.

Example 88. "Berceuse" from *Cinq Poèmes de Max Jacob*, measures 1–4 and 71–74. Copyright 1931 by Salabert, Paris. Used by permission.

In "Marc Chagall," already noted, a short postlude introduces four measures of a new motive which was not used before.

In "Berceuse" from *Cinq Poèmes de Max Jacob*, which starts without any prelude, the postlude consists of the beginning theme, bars 1–4 of the song (Example 88).

"Voyage" from *Calligrammes*, also without prelude, has an extended postlude with new material. The two thematic lines of this section are, in spite of the low dynamics (*ppp*) and the veiled pedal sound, doubled in octaves in both hands (Example 89).

However, the majority of postludes are only extended cadences, often based on interesting harmonies especially selected for this purpose.

The interludes, invariably short, either repeat part of the previous phrase, echolike or transposed, or, in other cases, anticipate the following phrase. Their function is connective and serves to provide a breathing spell for the singer. Only rarely does a whole melodic phrase appear between sections of a song, such as the eight bars of waltz in the piano part in "Voyage à Paris" from *Banalités* (Example 90).

Two special cases may be mentioned where instrumental prelude and postlude not only are set apart, but alternate with vocal bars or where the new piano melody is preceded, interrupted, or followed by short vocal interjections. This practice is similar to the accompanied recitatives in operas, especially by Mozart.

The first example is "enfant de Troupe" from *Cocardes*, in which the beginning eighteen bars show this technique. The main part of the song is entirely different. The complete material of the independent prelude appears again as postlude (ten bars).

Example 89.   "Voyage" from *Cal-ligrammes*, measures 34–40. Copyright 1948 by Heugel, Paris. Used by permission.

Example 90.   "Voyage à Paris" from *Banalités*, measures 43–49. Copyright 1940 by Eschig, Paris. Used by permission.

In "Miel de Narbonne" from the same group, the recitative, interrupted by an independent piano motive, appears only in the beginning. Recitative is also included in the postlude; but here, the main theme of the second part of the song itself is quoted.

When we summarize the use of the piano accompaniment, the variety of devices again has to be emphasized. The combination of many of these in single songs is unique for Poulenc. A perfect example of this diversity is the song "Figure de force brûlante et farouche" from *Tel Jour Telle Nuit*. The whole song is only twenty-three bars long, and contains seven different techniques of accompaniment. It is explained here in its entirety.

Bars 1–5 (3/4, 2/4)	Short chords, respectively single notes in the left hand, three times repeated D-minor triads in the right hand resulting in the pattern constantly reiterated.
Bars 6–8 (4/4, 2/4)	Sixteenth-note ostinato figure; in the right hand, syncopated accented bass groups of two notes, in octaves also repeated in bass.
Bars 9–10 (4/4)	Groups of three eighth notes followed by an eighth-note rest in the very high register in the right hand. Syncopated very low bass octaves (B♭–G), also repeated in the left hand.

Bar 11	General pause.
Bars 12–14 (6/4)	Both hands in treble clef, the right doubling the voice melody an octave higher, the left ostinato (A–F); both hands in continuous quarter-note motion.
Bar 15	Left hand continues ostinato (A–F). Right hand short eighth notes with grace notes on accentuated beats.
Bar 16	Sudden change of register, right hand descending in full-chord quarter notes for almost four octaves; left hand three times repeated broken-chord ostinato in eighth notes: F A^b A^b F
Bars 17–18 (4/4)	Thirty-second-note arpeggio ostinato in right hand (last two beats, sixteenth notes). Left hand sixteenth-note arpeggio ostinato.
Bar 19 (3/4)	Motion slows down to eighth notes.
Bars 20–21 (3/4, 4/4)	Right hand ostinato D in unison with voice; left hand (high register treble clef) two chromatic notes (E^b—E) repeated. Sound very transparent but dissonant.

151   **Piano Accompaniment**

Bars 22–24	Sudden register change, sustained very low bass and upper note
(4/4)	of right hand. Upper middle voice ostinato: C#–G, lower middle
	voice: E♭–D, in eighth notes. Melody then appears in lower middle
	voice leading to cadential D-major chord in last measure (Bar 24).

Poulenc conceived all his accompaniments not separately, but as units with the melody and the poem. Avoiding stereotypes, the piano either provides support for the voice note-by-note or strikes a different course. Consistency is never characteristic for Poulenc, an observation borne out again in the study of his accompanimental techniques. Certain and ever present, however, are the equal demands upon singer and pianist. The piano accompaniments are challenging but rewarding, rich in material that complements the poetry and supports the singer. Integrated with the poetic lines in a masterful way, they constitute some of the best of Poulenc's writing.

Notes

1. Bernac, *Interpretation of French Song*, 270.

2. Hell, *Francis Poulenc*, 3–4.

Epilogue

The microanalysis in the previous chapters has shown the various techniques which Poulenc used in his musical vocabulary in melody, harmony, and structure. All of his songs reveal his love of the human voice and its capacity to interpret the text in the spirit of the poet. He never disregarded the form nor the content of the poem. This is more remarkable as the styles of his main literary models were so varied. In spite of the fact that his favorite contemporaries—Guillaume Apollinaire, Paul Eluard, and Max Jacob—wrote in different poetic languages, he adapted his music perfectly to each of them. The same is true for his selection of other minor modern French poets or texts from the sixteenth century, or even folklike words in the Polish songs. Maybe the diversity, even inconsistency, of his music may be explained by this fact, its identification with different literary models.

This versatility is also the basis of Poulenc's melodic style. Simple direct melodies in regular phrase groups and periods alternate with mixtures of recitativelike declamation. Voice lines in small intervals are as common as large leaps and wide melodic curves, again according to the demands of the poems. If there is a sustained mood without much tension, lyric expansion is found in the music. If violent contrasts occur in the words, short irregular motives are found in which the diatonic intervals are often abandoned. The rhythm also is different according to the character of the text. Long extended lines in equal note values retained throughout a whole song are as frequent as the irregular sections with changing meter and note values. Frequent is the declamatory handling of the melody approaching the spoken word. Dynamic and melodic climaxes appear often in short succession, emphasizing the miniature character in many songs. The melodic tension and relaxation are determined by musical phrases, not by the verses. Proper prosody is always used in Poulenc's settings. The melodic line is never without primary importance.

The harmony also is subject to changes according to the mood of the poem. Though the traditional technique of diatonicism is maintained, it is embellished by unexpected sonorities, even modern complex chords containing simultaneous consonances and dissonances. Tonality is never abandoned, though sometimes shifting. Juxtaposition of keys is preferred to gradual modulations. Cadences are mostly conventional, though added color tones, even polytonality, often adds spice to the expected chords. The nonharmonic tones are used in a rather conventional way; also conventional is the treatment of added sonorities to simple harmonies. In general, Poulenc's harmonic vocabulary is selective with strong leaning to the usual tertian formations in well-approved organization.

Poulenc is not an innovator of new musical structures. The established patterns of the closed musical forms appear everywhere—binary, ternary, and even songs in one section. They are used mostly in their original way; the longer pieces are composites, as every section of the larger organization is subdivided so that those of smaller binary or ternary units are combined and mixed. The dimensions are variable. Their irregular length makes the conventional divisions more interesting. Strophic organization is only used in the folk-songs, but through-composed pieces are frequent. These can be sub-divided into different adjacent sections, or continue without any break. As the majority of Poulenc's songs are short, complicated formal organization is absent. However, the composer is able through application of slight variations to avoid structural monotony.

The same is true for his treatment of the piano. There are numerous accompaniment figures taken from the song literature of the nineteenth century—for instance, chord repetitions, arpeggios, and scale figures. But, their application is never without taste and subject to subtle, individual treatment. The fact that these devices are used in constant changes and in various nuances contributes to the feeling of originality in spite of certain repetition. Virtuosic piano writing in many songs and the use of color and sound in all, makes the style personal. Changes in motion and tempo and sensitive pedalling add to the charm of the music.

Though many songs show casualness and elegance, there are quite a few revealing depth and true sentiment. Among the over 140 songs are only a few quite alike, which speaks for the ingenuity of the composer.

Like the horticulturist who grafts young shoots on old branches to achieve abundant fruit, Poulenc builds on the traditional song literature to achieve a new flowering. He succeeded in giving rebirth to the French mélodie in the early twentieth century.

Bibliography

Aubry, Pierre, ed. *Les Plus Anciens Monuments de la musique française*. Mélanges de musicologie critique, IV (repr. of Paris, 1905 ed.). New York: Broude Brothers, 1969.

Austin, William W. *Music in the 20th Century from Debussy through Stravinsky*. New York: W. W. Norton & Co., 1966.

Bauer, Marion. *Twentieth Century Music*. Rev. ed. New York: G. P. Putnam Sons, 1947.

Bernac, Pierre. *The Interpretation of French Song*. New York: Praeger Publishers, Inc., 1970.

———. *Francis Poulenc The Man & his Songs*. New York: W. W. Norton & Co., Inc., 1977.

Candieu, Martine. "Duo avec Francis Poulenc." *Nouvelles littéraires* (May 4, 1961), 4–9.

Cocteau, Jean. *Le Groupe des Six*, Phonodisc, Program Notes, Angel Records 35117–118, "Introductory Speech, November, 6–10, 1953.

———. *Avric*, Georges, A Personal Memoir.

———. Dumesnil, René, The Six.

Collaer, Paul. *A History of Modern Music*. Translated by Sally Abeles. Cleveland: World Publishing Co., 1961.

Cooper, Martin. *French Music from the Death of Berlioz to the Death of Fauré*. London: Oxford University Press, 1951.

Demuth, Norman. *Musical Trends in the Twentieth Century*. London: Rockliff, 1952.

Deutsch, Babette. *Poetry Handbook; a Dictionary of Terms*. 3rd ed. New York: Funk & Wagnall's, 1969.

Durey, Louis. "Francis Poulenc." *The Chesterian*, New Series, No. 25 (September, 1922), 1–4.

Earle, Anita. Record Notes, *Francis Poulenc 1899–1963*. Phillips Records, PHS 900–148.

Eluard, Paul. *Selected Writings*, with English translation by Lloyd Alexander. New York: New Directions.

Fowlie, Wallace. *Mid-Century French Poets*. New York: Twayne Pub., 1955.

Gelatt, Roland. "A Vote for Francis Poulenc." *Saturday Review*, XXXIII/4 (January 28, 1950), 57–58.

Gruen, John. "Poulenc." *Musical America*, LXXX/5 (April, 1960), 6–7, 26–27.

Guthrie, Ramon, and George E. Diller, eds. *Prose and Poetry of Modern France*. New York: Scribner & Sons, 1964.

Hall, James Husst. *The Art Song*. Norman, Okla.: University of Oklahoma Press, 1953.

Hell, Henri. *Francis Poulenc, musicien français*. Paris: Librairie Plon, 1958; trans. Edward Lockspeiser, London: John Calder, 1959; New York, Grove Press, 1959.

Hughes, Allen. "Francis Poulenc, 1899–1963." *Musical America*, LXXXIII/2 (February, 1963), 20.

Jacobson, Robert. Record Notes, *Songs of Poulenc;* Gerard Souzay and Dalton Baldwin. RCA Victor, LSC-3018.

Kolodin, Irving. "The Merit of Poulenc." *Saturday Review*, XLVI/8 (February 23, 1963), 49–50, 66.

Lockspeiser, Edward. "The Wit and the Heart: A Study of Francis Poulenc." *High Fidelity*, VIII/7 (July, 1958), 35–37, 91–92.

Matthews, J. H. *Surrealist Poetry in France*. Syracuse, N.Y.: Syracuse University Press, 1969.

Milhaud, Darius. *Notes Without Music*. Translated by Donald Evans; edited by Rollo H. Meyers. New York: Alfred A. Knopf, 1953.

Nobel, Felix de. "Herinneringen aan Francis Poulenc." *Mens en Melodie*, XVIII (1963). English translation: "Memories of Francis Poulenc." *Sonorum Speculum*, 15 (1963), 39.

Ober, William B. Record Notes, *Poulenc Songs*. Westminster Records, WST 17105.

Poulenc, Francis. "A propos d'une lettre d'Arthur Honegger." *SMz*, CII (1962), 160.

———. *Correspondance 1915–1962*, réunie par Hélène de Wendel. Préface de Darius Milhaud. Paris: Editions du Seuil, 1967.

———. *Emmanuel Chabrier*. Paris: La Palatine, 1961.

———. "Entretiens avec Claude Rostand." Lecture in Paris, 1954, and at Juilliard School of Music, New York, 1956.

———. "Feuilles américaines." *Table ronde*, XXX (1950). Excerpts translated in *Composers on Music*, edited by Sam Morgenstern. New York: Pantheon, 1956, 514.

———. "Mes mélodies et leurs poètes." *Les Annales Conferencia*, XXXVI (1947).

———. "Moi et mes amis; Confidences recueilles par Stéphane Audel." Radio interviews, publ. Paris: La Palatine, 1963.

———. "Mon ami Honegger." *Journal musical français*, September 27, 1963.

———. "Paris Notes." *Fanfare*, London, 1921.

Rašín, Vera. "Les Six and Jean Cocteau." *Music and Letters*, XXXVIII/2 (April, 1957), 164–69.

Rorem, Ned. "Poulenc—A Memoir." *Tempo* (Spring, 1963), 28–29.

Rostand, Claude. "Visages de Poulenc." *Revue musical de la Suisse romande* (April, 1963).

Roy, Jean. *Francis Poulenc: l'homme et son oeuvre*. Paris: Editions Seghers, 1964.

Sabin, Robert. "Poulenc: The Essence is Simplicity." *Musical America*, LXIX (November 15, 1949), 27.

Schaeffner, André. "Francis Poulenc, musicien français." *Contrepoints*, I (1946).

Shapiro, Karl, and Robert Beum. *A Prosody Handbook*. New York: Harper & Row, 1965.

Shattuck, Roger. *The Banquet Years*. New York: Random House, 1968.

———, ed. and trans. *Selected Writings of Guillaume Apollinaire*. New York: New Directions, 1971.

Steegmuller, Francis. *Apollinaire Poet Among the Painters*. New York: Farrar, Straus and Co., 1963.

Thorlby, A. K., ed. *The Penguin Companion to Literature* (European), Baltimore: Penguin Books, 1969.

Trickey, Samuel Mueller. "Les Six." Ph.D. dissertation, North Texas State University, 1955.

Vein, Irving. "Francis Poulenc." *The Chesterian*, XXIX (July, 1954), 179.

Werner, Warren Kent. "The Harmonic Style of Francis Poulenc." Ph.D. dissertation, University of Iowa, 1966.

Catalogue of the Published Songs of Francis Poulenc*

YEAR	TITLE	PUBLISHER
1918/19	Le Bestiaire ou Cortège d'Orphée (G. Apollinaire) (1) Le dromadaire; (2) La chèvre du Thibet; (3) La sauterelle; (4) Le dauphin; (5) L'écrevisse; (6) La carpe	Max Eschig
1919	Cocardes (Jean Cocteau) (1) Miel de Narbonne; (2) Bonne d'enfant; (3) Enfant de troupe	Max Eschig
1924/25	Poèmes de Ronsard (1) Attributs; (2) Le tombeau; (3) Ballet; (4) Je n'ai plus que les os; (5) A son page	Heugel

* This listing is the one given in Pierre Bernac's *The Interpretation of French Song*. It postdates Henri Hell's listing in his book *Francis Poulenc*.

YEAR	TITLE	PUBLISHER
1926	Chansons Gaillardes (Anonymous seventeenth-century text) (1) La maîtresse volage; (2) Chanson à boire; (3) Madrigal; (4) Invocation aux Parques; (5) Couplets bachiques; (6) L'offrande; (7) La belle jeunesse; (8) Sérénade	Heugel
1927	Vocalise (Anonymous)	Leduc
1927/28	Airs chantés (J. Moréas) (1) Air romantique; (2) Air champêtre; (3) Air grave; (4) Air vif	Salabert
1930	Épitaphe (Malherbe)	Salabert
1931	Trois poèmes de Louise Lalanne (G. Apollinaire) (1) Le présent; (2) Chanson; (3) Hier	Salabert
1931	Quatre poèmes (G. Apollinaire) (1) L'anguille; (2) Carte postale; (3) Avant le cinéma; (4) 1904	Salabert
1931	Cinq Poèmes (Max Jacob) (1) Chanson bretonne; (2) Le cimetière; (3) La petite servante; (4) Berceuse; (5) Souric et Mouric	Salabert

YEAR	TITLE	PUBLISHER
1934	Huit Chansons Polonaises (1) La couronne; (2) Le départ; (3) Les gars polonais; (4) Le dernier Mazour; (5) L'adieu; (6) Le drapeau blanc; (7) La Vistule; (8) Le Lac	Salabert
1935	Cinq Poèmes (Paul Eluard) (1) Peut-il se reposer? (2) Il la prend dans ses bras; (3) Plume d'eau claire; (4) Rôdeuse au front de verre; (5) Amoureuses	Durand
1935	A sa guitare (Ronsard)	Durand
1937	Tel jour telle nuit (P. Eluard) (1) Bonne journée; (2) Une ruine coquille vide; (3) Le front comme un drapeau perdu; (4) Une roulotte couverte en tuiles; (5) A toutes brides; (6) Une herbe pauvre; (7) Je n'ai envie que de t'aimer; (8) Figure de force brûlante et farouche; (9) Nous avons fait la nuit	Durand
1937	Trois poèmes (Louise de Vilmorin) (1) Le garçon de Liège; (2) Au-delà; (3) Aux officiers de la Garde Blanche	Durand

YEAR	TITLE	PUBLISHER
1938	Deux Poèmes (G. Apollinaire) (1) Dans le jardin d'Anna; (2) Allons, plus vite	Salabert
1938	Miroirs brûlants (P. Eluard) (1) Tu vois le feu du soir; (2) Miroirs brûlants	Salabert
1938	Le portrait (Colette)	Salabert
1938	La grenouillère (G. Apollinaire)	Salabert
1938	Priez pour paix (Charles d'Orléans)	Salabert
1938	Ce doux petit visage (P. Eluard)	Salabert
1939	Bleuet (G. Apollinaire)	Durand
1939	Fiançailles pour rire (Lousie de Vilmorin) (1) La dame d'André; (2) Dans l'herbe; (3) Il vole; (4) Mon cadavre est doux comme un gant; (5) Violon; (6) Fleurs	Salabert
1940	Banalités (G. Apollinaire) (1) Chanson d'Orkenise; (2) Hôtel; (3) Fagnes de Wallonie; (4) Voyage à Paris; (5) Sanglots	Max Eschig

YEAR	TITLE	PUBLISHER
1942	Chansons villageoises (Maurice Fombeure) (1) Chanson du clair tamis; (2) Les gars qui vont à la fête; (3) C'est le joli printemps; (4) Le mendiant; (5) Chanson de la fille frivole; (6) Le retour du sergent	Max Eschig
1943	Métamorphoses (Louise de Vilmorin) (1) Reine des mouettes; (2) C'est ainsi que tu es; (3) Paganini	Salabert
1943	Deux Poèmes (L. Aragon) (1) C.; (2) Fêtes galantes	Salabert
1945	Montparnasse (G. Apollinaire)	Max Eschig
1945	Hyde Park (G. Apollinaire)	Max Eschig
1946	Le pont (G. Apollinaire)	Max Eschig
1946	Un poème (G. Appollinaire)	Max Eschig
1946	Paul et Virginie (Raymond Radiguet)	Max Eschig
1947	Mais mourir (P. Eluard)	Heugel
1947	Hymne (Racine)	Salabert

163 **Appendix**

YEAR	TITLE	PUBLISHER
1947	Trois chansons de Garcia-Lorca (1) L'enfant muet; (2) Adelina à la promenade; (3) Chanson de l'oranger sec	Heugel
1947	Le disparu (Robert Desnos)	Salabert
1947	Main dominée par le coeur (P. Eluard)	Salabert
1948	Calligrammes (G. Apollinaire) (1) L'espionne; (2) Mutation; (3) Vers le Sud; (4) Il pleut; (5) La grâce exilée; (6) Aussi bien que les cigales; (7) Voyage	Heugel
1949	Mazurka (Louise de Vilmorin) (dans: Mouvements du coeur)	Heugel
1950	La Fraîcheur et le Feu (P. Eluard) (1) Rayon des yeux . . . ; (2) Le matin les branches attisent . . . ; (3) Tout disparut . . . ; (4) Dans les ténèbres du jardin . . . ; (5) Unis la fraîcheur et le feu . . . ; (6) Homme au sourire tendre . . . ; (7) La grande rivière qui va . . .	Max Eschig
1954	Parisiana (Max Jacob) (1) Jouer du bugle; (2) Vous n'écrivez plus?	Salabert

YEAR	TITLE	PUBLISHER
1954	Rosemonde (G. Apollinaire)	Max Eschig
1956	Le travail du peintre (P. Eluard) (1) Pablo Picasso; (2) Marc Chagall; (3) Georges Braque; (4) Juan Gris; (5) Paul Klee; (6) Joan Miro; (7) Jacques Villon	Max Eschig
1956	Deux mélodies 1956 (1) La souris (G. Apollinaire); (2) Nuage (Laurence de Beylié)	Max Eschig
1956	Dernier poème (Robert Desnos)	Max Eschig
1958	Une chanson de porcelaine (P. Eluard)	Max Eschig
1960	La courte paille (Maurice Carême) (1) Le sommeil; (2) Quelle aventure!; (3) La reine de coeur; (4) Ba, be, bi, bo, bu; (5) Les anges musiciens; (6) Le carafon; (7) Lune d'Avril	Max Eschig

Index to the Songs of Poulenc & the Poets

General Index